GREAT AMERICAN HEROES

GREAT AMERICAN HEROES

BY JEAN FIEDLER

ILLUSTRATED BY RAYMOND BURNS

Hart Publishing Company, Inc.

NEW YORK CITY

Manufactured in the United States of America

CONTENTS

List of Illustrations

ROGER WILLIAMS
Pioneer of Religious Freedom

In 1631, men, women, and children, some dressed in rags, others in the simplest clothes, were standing on the deck of the *Lyon,* a schooner that had sailed from Bristol, England. Bundles were thrown all around—the meager and pitiful belongings of these immigrants who had just set out for Massachusetts in the New World—America.

They had left behind them relatives, friends, and their old way of life. Now they were going to a pioneer land. Most of them had uprooted themselves—not to seek wealth, nor power, nor adventure—but rather to find freedom from religious persecution.

Roger Williams and his wife were among them. Roger stood on the deck and proclaimed: "Each man must find his own way to God. I shall fight for freedom as long as I live!"

Williams was then a young preacher of twenty-seven. In England, he had been summoned to court to account for his so-called wild preachings. Now he and his wife were fleeing their birthplace to escape imprisonment in the Tower of London where heretics were jailed, hanged, or beheaded. Williams had had the nerve to say that everybody should have a right to his own religious beliefs. The Church of England and even the Crown considered this downright heresy—an attempt to undermine church and state authority.

Even before Roger Williams was a teenager, he dreamed of religious freedom. He was born in England in 1604. He had witnessed the abuses inflicted upon the Puritans by King James. The suffering of the persecuted had a deep effect on him; he was determined to do something about bigotry when he became a man.

What disappointment greeted young Roger Williams when he set foot in the New World! In America, he found the laws stricter than they were in England. Men were even imprisoned for fishing on Sunday. The whole colony of Boston, still joined to the Church of England in its beliefs, allowed no religious freedom.

Unwilling to submit to such oppression, the young preacher again proclaimed from the pulpit: "Every person must have the opportunity to find his own way to God!"

Because of his beliefs, the elders of Boston ordered Williams driven out of the New World and sent back to England.

Williams decided to escape, this time to what is now known as Rhode Island. In bitter cold weather, he and a cousin set out on foot to seek a safe place.

Roger Williams had been kind to the Indians, had learned their many languages, traded with them, and had smoked the pipe of peace with the redmen. The Indians, in turn, were kind to him, sheltered him, fed him, and sold him land.

The terrain which the Indians sold to Roger Williams was to become known as Rhode Island. Here began the commencement of religious freedom in America.

Roger Williams proclaimed, "God has led us here. Let us call this place Providence." And since that day, Providence has been the capital of Rhode Island.

Roger Williams wrote: "Papists and Protestants Jews and Turks, may go aboard one ship. The Captain never interferes with the religious faiths of any aboard, and neither will I. All are welcome here. I shall fight for religious freedom as long as I live."

People everywhere heard of this fearless man who wanted to practice his own beliefs and permit others do the same. Soon, Roger Williams was joined by members of other faiths. Log cabins were built; farms were cultivated; a democratic government was set up. The colony

Log cabins were built . . .

of Rhode Island became a haven for all the oppressed.

Scornfully, some people called Rhode Island "Rogues' Island;" others called it "The sink of New England." But Roger Williams never swerved in his determination. He lived to a ripe old age, secure in the knowledge that he was doing the Lord's work.

JOHN PETER ZENGER

Champion of Freedom of the Press

Thirteen-year-old Peter Zenger watched anxiously as his mother wrote her name on the paper. Then Mr. Bradford signed his name, and the transaction was completed. John Peter Zenger had now been legally indentured for eight years as an apprentice of William Bradford, Printer.

As soon as Mrs. Zenger had gone, Peter's new master said, "Come, boy, and I will show you where we do our work."

Peter followed Mr. Bradford into the workroom. The two presses were busily running. On high wires hung newly printed sheets of paper drying before they could be stacked. Piles of paper were in every corner. Peter stood at the type tray looking with awe at the small metal pieces of type. Combinations of these letters made words. Soon he would learn to print whole sentences.

To escape religious persecution, Peter's family had fled from his birthplace in Germany to the Netherlands, and then once again to England, and finally to the Colony of New York in America. Here the Zengers hoped to settle for good.

After he had learned the printing trade, Peter married and then got a job as a full-fledged printer with Mr. Bradford.

The fact that Mr. Bradford decided to publish a newspaper was mighty pleasing to young Zenger. But Peter soon came to realize that Mr. Bradford would not take the risk of offending the government authorities; and as a consequence; the *New York Gazette* was dull, mild in tone, and contained little of interest. This was not Peter's idea of what a newspaper should be.

So, as Peter had saved money, he enlisted the help of two prominent men in town to set up a printing business; James Alexander, a lawyer, and Lewis Morris, Jr., the son of the Chief Justice of the Supreme Court, became his backers.

At that time, gossip centered around the new Governor appointed by the British Crown, a Colonel William Cosby. Almost upon his arrival, the new Governor demonstrated his arrogance. People talked with distaste of his bad temper and his strong greed. A story made the rounds about the punishment meted out to a farmer whose cart had blocked the path of the Governor's carriage. Cosby had ordered the man severely horse-whipped. Although the so-called offender had barely escaped death, there was no authority to whom he dared to turn to complain. Other rumors were rife about the Governor's having stolen a deed to land, and about his having extracted bribes.

As injustice followed injustice, the Colony of New York was horrified to learn that Governor Cosby had expelled Chief Justice Morris from the Supreme Court. This meant that the Governor could order the arrest of anyone on a trumped-up charge, and then appoint a judge to find the accused guilty.

In protest, Lewis Morris, Jr., and his friends formed a political organization called the Popular Party. James Alexander was to lead it. If ever the time had come for a newspaper to tell the people what was happening, it was now. Financed by Morris and other forward-looking citizens, Peter Zenger began publication of a newspaper which he called the *Weekly Journal.* One of its first articles concerned the election of an Assemblyman. The Popular Party had put up former Chief Justice Morris. Cosby, of course, put up his own man.

The Governor's henchmen tried in every which way to prevent lawful voters from exercising their rightful franchise; but nevertheless, Morris won the election. Furious, Governor Cosby vowed to get even.

No longer were the people of New York kept in the dark. Zenger's newspaper told the facts, and thundered against the Governor's tyranny. Zenger was threatened, but he still continued to publish. But soon the blow fell. He was arrested and put in jail. The Governor issued a proclamation offering a sizable reward to anyone who would tell the names of the men who wrote the articles for Peter Zenger's *Weekly Journal.* Needless to say, James Alexander, former Chief Justice Morris, and other prominent individuals of the Popular Party had written the articles. Despite their high position in the community, they might, if exposed, be found guilty of sedition and be hung.

At the trial, the defendants argued that the judge could not be fair since he had been appointed by Governor Cosby. The immediate response by the judge was to disbar the lawyers who questioned his impartiality. But an attempt by the prosecution to appoint jurors from among their own followers failed.

As the trial began, an old man entered the courtroom. He introduced himself to Judge Delancey as Andrew Hamilton. Everyone was startled, for Hamilton was known far and wide as an outstanding lawyer from Pennsylvania. He stated to the court that he had been admitted to practice in England. Though ill, this venerable gentleman had made the trip to New York to defend Peter Zenger. The advocate's contention was that the publication of the newspaper containing

. . . Hamilton addressed the jury . . .

matter which threw the Governor in a bad light was
not in itself a crime.

The prosecutor argued, any printed statement which
attacks a Governor is libel, but Hamilton was ready
to call witnesses who would offer positive proof of
Cosby's unlawful acts. Judge Delancey refused to ad-
mit such evidence in court.

When Hamilton addressed the jury, he said, "The
question before the court and you Gentlemen of the
Jury is not of small nor private concern. It is not the
cause of the poor printer, nor of New York alone,
which you are now trying. It may in its consequence
affect every free man in America. It is the *best* cause,
it is the cause of Liberty!"

Judge Delancey dismissed the jury to deliberate. He
had practically instructed them to find Peter Zenger
guilty of seditious libel. The jury returned, and the
court was breathless. The foreman rose to speak and
his voice rang out clearly: "We find the defendant,
Peter Zenger, not guilty!"

It was the most important victory for freedom of
speech and freedom of the press. And from this now-
famous case there began the long tradition that has
made Americans free to criticize their government, and
to publish, what each in good conscience believes to
be the truth.

BENJAMIN FRANKLIN
Master of Many Crafts

Young Ben Franklin gazed across Boston harbor. He loved everything about it—the smells of the salty sea, the majestic boats, the swarthy sailors who spoke in foreign tongues. How long he had wanted to be a sailor, he did not know; but the yearning seemed to be connected with his brother, Josiah, who had run away to sea.

Ben sighed unhappily. He knew his father hated seafaring. When Ben was eight, his father had said to him, "I hope you will enter the ministry; no man can have a finer calling."

Ben had gone to school with the idea that someday he would become a minister. But at the end of two years, his father sadly told him, "I'm afraid your schooling must stop, my son. Although our candle shop does fairly well, what I earn doesn't even provide the necessities for our family." His father spoke the truth. Of 17 children, 13 were still his father's financial responsibility.

The boy listened to his father respectfully. "Ben, I want you to work in the shop with me. There will be time for us to look around, and decide later about a career for you."

"One thing more," Josiah Franklin said, "You must promise me that when things grow difficult, you will not run away to sea as your brother did."

Ben stifled a groan. This was exactly what he had so often dreamed of doing. But young Ben said, "I promise, sir, I won't run away to sea."

All this had happened two years ago. Now, as he stood staring out at the harbor, Ben was 12 and on the verge of an important event. This very day, he was to begin a nine-year apprenticeship to his brother, James, who owned a printing shop. At least, Ben tried to console himself, a printing shop would be free of the thick odor of tallow. And who knew? In time, he might like the printing trade. So, after a longing glance at the harbor, Ben turned and went off to begin his future.

The first days in the printing shop tried Ben's patience. "I'll show you no favoritism because you're my brother," James Franklin told him immediately.

"You're to do exactly what I tell you."

Ben subdued the quick rebellion that surged through him at his brother's manner. He said nothing, merely nodding his head.

Quickly, he learned to wash type. After that, when James handed him a composing stick and gave him his first lesson in typesetting, Ben had a moment's pleasure. He actually liked setting type. He handled the type skillfully, neither fumbling nor spilling type from the fonts. The sheets he printed were clean; the type accurate.

Since James was not married, he and his apprentices ate their meals in a private home near the shop. One night at dinner, Ben discovered that one of the boarders worked in a bookstore. "Lucky you!" he exclaimed.

"Why am I so lucky?" The other boy seemed puzzled.

"You can read all the books in the store."

"I haven't read even one. I don't like to read," the boy replied. "But if you do, I'll bring you a book tonight. Be sure to have it back here by tomorrow morning. And you must keep it clean."

"Oh, I'll be careful of it," Ben promised, delighted at this stroke of luck.

He found that the books he read increased his desire to read more. But Ben had no money to buy books.

One day, he read a book which advised giving up the eating of meat. He decided to try this new diet, but eating at the boarding house presented obstacles. Then, Ben came up with an idea. He could hardly wait to tell James.

"If you give me half the money you pay for my food," he began eagerly, "I'll provide my own meals and you needn't bother about me."

"Sounds all right," James agreed.

Ben's plan was to save money on food and to buy books with the difference. He ate no meat and lived mostly on raisins and bread and water. Although his body was poorly nourished, his mind and imagination fed on each new volume he read.

He found and saved bits and pieces of wax. Making his own candles, he read by candlelight such different books as: *Pilgrim's Progress, Plutarch's Lives,* Cotton Mather's *Essays to Do Good,* and Defoe's *Robinson Crusoe.* In addition, he taught himself arithmetic— which he had failed in school; then algebra, geometry, navigation, grammar, and logic.

Reading, in turn, made Ben want to write. He began teaching himself to write by reading some piece of material and then rewriting the piece in his own words.

As his writing improved, Ben longed to see his own work in print. By this time, James Franklin was printing his own newspaper, *The New England Courant.* But Ben knew that if he revealed his desire to James, his brother would scornfully laugh him off. First, thought Ben, I'll write what I want to say, and then

I'll see if I can find a way to have it printed.

He did just that. In the middle of the night, Ben slipped a bundle of papers under the door of his brother's print shop. Then he turned, and ran quickly up to bed.

In the morning, Ben watched as his brother began to read the sheets found under the door. "Well," said James Franklin, "a lady by the name of Silence Dogood wants to become a contributor of ours. I wonder what she has to say."

As he read on, James' chuckles became more and more frequent. "Excellent," he said looking pleased, "she writes well and she has wit. She is obviously a shrewd lady. She leaves her reader in the middle of an interesting episode and says, 'more tomorrow'." "Here, set them up."

Ben turned away to hide the delighted grin on his face. His plan had worked. As the anonymous lady, Silence Dogood, Ben saw his work published, and he enjoyed the public reactions. The readers of *The Courant* were delighted with the whimsical wit of Silence Dogood and eagerly looked forward to each day's episode.

Eventually, Ben confessed that he was the author of the articles. His brother James was furious at the deception. Relations between the brothers grew strained. Ben's imagination and intelligence irritated James; Ben, in turn, grew more and more rebellious at the abusive treatment he suffered at his brother's hands.

After one particularly bitter quarrel, Ben decided to do something. Complaining to his father would be useless. Having apprenticed the boy to James until Ben would be 21, Josiah Franklin would not go back on his word.

Ben decided to run away. He traveled to New York, but there was no work for him as a printer in that small city. One kindly man whom he met, a Mr. Bradford, advised Ben to try Philadelphia.

By the time he reached Philadelphia, Ben was starving. Finding a bake shop, Ben went in and spent three pennies for three huge rolls. As he was eating one, he passed a young girl standing on her porch. The girl saw a young man, disheveled, laden with books, munching on an enormous roll. They exchanged glances. Bursting into laughter, the girl turned and went into the house. 'I must look a sight,' Ben thought. The girl was Deborah Read—later to become Ben's wife and the mother of his two children.

It was Mr. Bradford's son who helped Ben get a job with the printer, Samuel Keimer. Recognizing immediately that Keimer's press needed repair, Ben quickly went to work on it. The printer was pleased with Ben from the beginning, and came to rely on him more and more. Soon, Ben had the responsibility for printing the entire newspaper.

Word of his skill spread far and wide. One after-

noon, Ben was surprised to learn that the Governor
of Pennsylvania, Sir William Keith, wanted to talk with
him. The Governor had a plan. He wanted to estab-
lish Ben in his own printing business and hoped Ben's
father would supply some of the money. Ben's father
felt that, at 18, Ben was too young to assume such a
responsibility, so the Governor offered to supply the
money himself.

Bursting into laughter, the girl turned and
went into the house.

"Go to London," he told Ben, "and buy the printing equipment you will need. The money will be waiting for you aboard ship."

Ben brimming with expectations, boarded a ship and set sail for London. Unfortunately, the Governor did not keep his word; there was no money for Ben. When the ship docked, Ben found himself in London, almost penniless and with no one to turn to. However, his boundless curiosity and interest in everyone and everything saved him. Ben soon made friends, and finally found work with a printer.

While in London, Ben met Thomas Denham, a Quaker merchant, with whom he became friendly. Den-

ham suggested Ben return to Philadelphia with him to work in his store. This unexpected opportunity interested Ben for he had grown to respect and admire the older man.

And so, a year and a half after he landed in England, Ben went back to Philadelphia. He was determined to learn selling and accounting. He studied nights, and he progressed rapidly. But then an unexpected tragedy struck. Both Ben and Mr. Denham became terribly ill. Ben's youthful strength helped him recover, but his good friend, Mr. Denham, died—leaving Franklin a small legacy.

Once more Ben had to start from the beginning. His old employer, Samuel Keimer, hired Ben as a printer.

Some time later, Ben and a friend, Hugh Meredith, opened a printing house of their own, financed by Meredith's father. In 1729, the *Pennsylvania Gazette* was published for the first time. It was later to become the *Saturday Evening Post*.

Now that Ben was part owner of a newspaper, he could print his own work freely. His wit and good sense pleased his readers. Gradually, his name became known throughout the colonies.

In 1730, Ben Franklin married the laughing girl whom he had seen his first day in Philadelphia—Deborah Read. Soon afterwards, Ben asked his wife, "What do you think of my printing a new almanac?"

Few homes were without an almanac in those days

—a small booklet which gave calendar dates, information about the stars, tides, and other facts. Debby was
not certain. "There are so many almanacs already in
print," she protested.

"Yes," said Ben, "but not like the one I have in
mind."

He was already visualizing the form his almanac
would take. It would be small and have a pale green
cover with pink and red flowers. Franklin went on
to imagine a mythical man, named Richard, who would
write the almanac. Richard would take on the work
because he was poor and needed money for his extrava-
gant wife. From Richard's pen, wise and witty sayings
would pour out to influence. readers in habits of thrift
and honest living. Franklin turned this vision into
reality when he wrote and published *Poor Richard's
Almanac*. It was an instant success. In time, people came
to love Poor Richard and to guide their lives by his wise
sayings.

Along with his other interests, Ben founded a dis-
cussion group which he named the *Junto*. Its members
were devoted to the improvement of reading, speaking,
and thinking. In time, the *Junto* grew into the American Philosophical Society.

Ben's constant love for .books led to his founding
the first circulating library in America. He also estab-
lished the first fire department, the first American fire
insurance company, and an educational institution, The

Academy, which later became the University of Pennsylvania.

At 42, Ben Franklin had earned enough money to retire. His philosophy about money was a simple one. "A wise man will desire no more than what he may get justly, use soberly, distribute cheerfully, leave cautiously."

It was after his retirement that Ben's genius shone even more brightly than it had before. He now had the leisure to use his keen intelligence in the service of humanity.

For some years, his interest in electricity had occupied his thoughts. He had read and studied and come to the conclusion that lightning is electricity. In 1754, he flew a specially rigged kite in a thunderstorm. To the kite, he attached a wire on which was fastened a key. When lightning struck the wire, the lightning traveled to the key, struck it, and caused a spark. In this way, Franklin proved his theory.

He also invented a stove with improved heating power. People said of the Franklin stove, "It keeps us warmer and even saves fuel!"

When he was approached by business men to take out patents for his inventions, he refused. "My inventions," Ben Franklin said, "are for the good of mankind."

Before his retirement, Franklin had held the position of Clerk of the Pennsylvania Assembly. In 1753, he

. . . he flew a specially rigged kite in a thunderstorm.

was appointed Post Master General of all the colonies. While he served in that office, he reorganized the postal system, making it self-supporting for the first time. He also took measures to increase the speed of delivery, and to insure the safety of the mail and of the carriers.

During the French and Indian War, Franklin, largely at his own expense, obtained wagons and supplies for General Braddock who was then defending the colonies. Franklin's title was Colonel of the Philadelphia Militia.

In 1757, the Pennsylvania Assembly found itself involved in a quarrel between England and Philadelphia. A man of rare diplomacy was needed to settle the dispute. Ben Franklin was chosen. In the exchanges which followed, he impressed all those who met him. As a result, Ben was to spend the greater part of the next 18 years in England acting as a peacemaker.

Largely through his efforts, the Stamp Act, which had aroused so much anger in the colonies, was repealed.

When he returned to America in 1775, a sad loss awaited him. His wife, Debby, had died during his absence. The blow stunned him. But his country's dilemma took precedence over his personal sorrow. Important work awaited him. At the age of 70, Ben plunged into the difficult job of protecting the country.

A member of the Second Continental Congress, he helped to draft the Declaration of Independence; later, he was one of its signers. During the signing ceremonies he made everyone chuckle when he said, "We must all hang together or assuredly we shall all hang separately."

The Colonial Congress sent him to France to seek aid. The French were greatly impressed by this sage man. In 1778, France, largely through the influence of Franklin, came into the Revolutionary War on the American side.

In his old age, Ben Franklin served as President of the Executive Council of Pennsylvania. At 81, he was named as a delegate to the Constitutional Convention, the oldest member there. He was the only man to sign all four of these historic documents: the Declaration of Independence, the Treaty of Alliance, the Treaty of Peace (which ended the American Revolution), and the Constitution of the United States of America.

Years before when, as a boy, Ben Franklin had gazed across the Boston harbor with longing, he could not have imagined he would become author, publisher, scientist, inventor, and statesman. Nor could he have dreamed that the first President of the United States, George Washington, would pay him tribute in these glowing words: "If to be venerated for benevolence, if to be admired for talents, if to be esteemed for patriotism, if to be loved for philanthropy can gratify the human mind—you must have the pleasing consolation to know that you have not lived in vain."

ISRAEL PUTNAM
Fighting Yankee Farmer

One spring night towards the end of the American Revolutionary War, two Yankee soldiers were standing guard in George Washington's camp. As they stood there, rifles in their hands, a figure came towards them in the darkness.

"Who goes there?" they called out, raising their guns.

"General Israel Putnam," came the answer.

"Oh, sorry, sir. It was too dark to recognize you. Good evening, sir."

"Good evening, boys. Nice night."

As the stout figure of General Putnam disappeared into the night, one of the soldiers said, "So that's Ol' Put! I've heard a lot about him. Must be about 57 by now—pretty old for a soldier!"

"Yep, he's at least 57 all right, but he's a better soldier than many men thirty years younger. Why, did you ever hear the story about how he escaped from a whole company of Redcoats in Connecticut last year?

"Seems he found out they were going to attack some little town up near the woods there, so he leaped right on his horse and was off like the wind, to warn the people in the town. But one of the Redcoats saw him, and right away, the whole British Company was after him.

"Well, their horses were fresher than his, so they pretty near caught him. But Old Put was too smart for them—too good a horseman, too. When they were nearly up to him, he turned off the main road down a little side path that ended on a cliff. The Redcoats followed right after, ready to bet King George's palace itself that they had him cornered. But they were in for some surprise! I'd give plenty to have seen their faces when they saw Old Put and his horse go right over the edge of that cliff! And I'd give a lot more to have seen how they looked when they got to the edge of it themselves, and saw Old Put, safe and sound, fifty feet below, galloping away down the road!"

"Well, what did he do—did he jump?"

"That's just what the British wanted to know," laughed the storyteller. "No, he didn't jump, but it took those Redcoats a mighty long time to find the path he used. It went right down the side of the cliff, by gosh! I saw the path myself—a narrow, rocky little trail, so steep I wouldn't want to *walk* down it! That was some risk for a man to take, especially a man his age! But Old Put's not afraid of anything!"

"Yep, you're right. Old Put's not afraid of anything! Why, when I was a little kid, he was famous among the farmers all over Connecticut.

"There was an old she-wolf who'd been killing sheep and goats on all the farms in his neighborhood. She was as fierce a creature as they come. Must have been a real fighter for she'd lost all the toes on one paw. They could tell that from the tracks she left. Well, one night she killed seventy of Old Put's sheep and goats. She didn't know it, but she was picking on the wrong man. Old Put just set his mind on getting her, and by gosh, he did, too, in the end, though it's a wonder he wasn't killed doing it.

"He and his neighbors tracked her down to a cave, about five miles away from his farm. They sent the dogs in after her, but the dogs came out yelping and bleeding. Then they spent almost the whole day trying to smoke her out. But she was stubborn and she wouldn't budge. Finally, about evening time, Old Put got sore. 'I'm going in after her,' he said. And that was all there was to it!

"It was black as pitch in that cave, and a man couldn't stand up in there, because it was too low. Everyone knew that the wolf was raging and raring to fight. But you couldn't stop Old Put. He just isn't afraid of anything. He had his neighbors tie a rope to his leg, so that they could pull him out in a hurry if they had to. Then, holding a torch in one hand, he crawled into the dark cave. Even with a torch, he could hardly see a thing. Suddenly, he heard a growl and saw two bright eyes gleaming at him in the darkness. He gave the signal to be pulled out, and his friends dragged him out so fast they nearly killed him.

"But don't think Old Put was giving up—not he, he was just returning for his gun. He went right back into that cave, this time crawling along with a rifle in one hand and a torch in the other. When he got up to the wolf, he could see she was furious. Just as she was about to spring, he fired his rifle. Then his friends pulled him out of the cave again. But Old Put's never satisfied until a job is done. He wanted to be sure that the wolf was dead and not just wounded. Wild horses couldn't drag *me* into a black cave alone with a wounded she-wolf, but I guess I'm not as brave as Old Put. He went back in there. and lucky for the Continental Army, the wolf was dead. He dragged her out after him to prove it!"

"Lucky for the Continental Army is right! Old Put's a real patriot. Why, they say when he heard that fighting had broken out against the British at Lexington, he was ploughing his field. He just let go of the plough right where it was, then got on a horse, and rode off to

He dragged her out to prove it!

Governor Trumbull for orders. Didn't waste a minute.

"Old Put's a man I'm going to tell my grandchildren about. If anyone ever gets around to writing a history book about this war, he'll be in there, all right, up near the first chapter."

And indeed, we Americans have remembered to this day the name of brave, old Israel Putnam.

PATRICK HENRY
Champion of American Freedom

During the American Revolution, the words of the fearless patriot, Patrick Henry, did as much to help us gain our liberty as the bravery of any soldier on the battlefield. For he was the man who first dared to say publicly what other men knew in their hearts—that the time had come when there was no other choice but to fight Great Britain for freedom.

All over America, men heard of Patrick Henry. His flaming words inspired them with the courage they needed to carry on the great struggle that lay ahead.

In March of the year 1775, a little group of men met secretly in a church in Richmond, Virginia. They were to decide whether or not to create an army with which to defend themselves against the British. Although the fighting had not yet started, everyone knew that it was likely that war lay ahead; and many people felt that they should be prepared for it. But there was still a large group who was afraid that the small, weak colonies could never be victorious against the armed might of England. Some of these men were at this meeting. They got up and had their say. Patrick Henry listened in silent anguish until they were finished. Then he arose, and with clenched fists and burning eyes, began to speak.

He spoke of the many injustices imposed by Great Britain, of the many peaceful ways in which the American colonies had tried to have these injustices corrected, of the letters and petitions they had sent, begging the English king to lower the harsh taxes he had forced on them, and of the scorn and growing tyranny with which these peaceful requests had been met. Finally, he spoke of the large number of soldiers Britain had just landed in America. These soldiers, Henry said, were not sent here in "love and friendship."

"Let us not deceive ourselves," he cried. "These are the implements of war and subjugation. If we wish to be free we must fight! I repeat it, sir—we must fight! An appeal to arms and to the God of Hosts is all that is left us.

"They tell us, sir, that we are weak—unable to cope with so formidable an adversary. But when shall we be stronger? Will it be the next week, or the next year?

". . . give me liberty, or give me death!"

Will it be when we are totally disarmed, and when a British guard shall be stationed in every house?

"Sir, we are not weak, if we make a proper use of those means which the God of nature hath placed in our power. The war is inevitable. And let it come! I repeat it, sir, let it come!

"Gentlemen may cry peace, peace, but there is no peace. The war is actually begun. The next gale that sweeps from the north will bring to our ears the clash of resounding arms. Our brethren are already in the field. Why stand we here idle? What is it that gentlemen wish? What would they have? Is life so dear, or peace so sweet, as to be purchased at the price of chains and slavery? Forbid it, Almighty God! I know not what course others may take, but as for me, give me liberty, or give me death!"

PAUL REVERE
Watchman of the American Revolution

The moon was full and brilliant. Bad luck that this should be a clear, cloudless night. As Paul Revere sat tense in the rear of his rowboat, the small craft passed within fifteen feet of the stern of the British gunship, Somerset. If any crewman on the English vessel just happened to peer down over the railing, it would be too bad for Paul and his two friends.

On they rowed, silently, slowly, their oarlocks muffled in flannel to avoid making noise. The blades of their oars were kept under water, so that the moonlight would not reflect off the wet wood. They speak to each other only in the very faintest of occasional whispers.

As the boat neared the far bank, Paul looked back toward Boston. He could see two lights shining from the steeple of Christ Church where Robert Newman, the sexton, had hung them earlier that night. Now he knew that the British planned their attack on that very night. The British attack had been expected for weeks, and the Americans had been on guard. The British had been patrolling every road; the only way Paul could reach his friends was to row across the bay.

When the boat scraped shore, Paul jumped into the shallow water, whispered farewell to his friends and silently made his way up along the shore, keeping to trees and bushes. Soon he came to a farmhouse. There in the front yard was a small group waiting for him.

"Thank God, you've made it." It was John Winters, a member of the Sons of Liberty, an organization that had been fighting the British. "There are British patrols all about, and they've instructions to let no one ride the roads tonight."

The English were well aware that Paul Revere had been one of the leaders of the American Colonists. George III, the British monarch, had refused to remove the high taxes on goods imported from England into the Colonies. The Colonists countered by not buying English articles. When the British king meant to force purchase, the Sons of Liberty had boarded the English ship and dumped every ounce of tea aboard the vessel into the Boston harbor.

Following the "Boston Tea Party" the English had become furious. That night they were making ready to attack Concord, Massachusetts, and capture the ammunition and guns the Sons of Liberty had stored there. It was Paul Revere's task to warn the Americans.

A young boy led out a sturdy, swift-footed horse onto the road.

"There she is, Paul, the fastest mare in the state. Good luck and Godspeed!" John Winters shook Paul's hand once more.

Paul swung himself into the saddle.

"Ride well!" his friends called. "Take care!"

Paul galloped off into the night. His mount was magnificent. He had never ridden such a horse before.

On he rode through the darkness, with the moon just bright enough to light up the road ahead of him. Suddenly, in the distance, he caught the flash of brass buttons. As he drew closer, he saw two Redcoats on horseback. They blocked his way.

"Halt!" cried the sentries. "Stop in the name of the King!"

With a shout of defiance, Paul turned his horse off the road. He rode on furiously. Paul glanced behind him, and saw that the horse of one of the Redcoats had stumbled. The rider was thrown to the ground. His companion pulled up, afraid to follow Paul alone through that blackness of forest.

Paul raced along. If he could just reach the first cluster of houses on the road to Lexington to spread the alarm, Concord would be saved.

"Arise! Arise! The British are coming!"

The little town of Medford appeared ahead through the trees. When he reached the first house, Paul reined his horse and jumped to the ground. He rapped on the window-pane with his riding crop. "Arise! Arise! The British are coming!" he shouted.

His words shattered the quiet of that sleeping town. Oil lamps were turned on, doors were thrown open. Men rubbed their tired eyes with one hand, and reached for rifles with the other.

But Paul rode on. As he left Medford, he saw the Minute Men already forming in the village square, making ready to march on to Concord where the final stand would be made.

At last, Paul reached Lexington. He alerted the entire town. He had not arrived any too soon. Before long, the feathered hats, the red coats, and the brass buttons of the British Regulars appeared along the road. A line of half-armed men had been stationed here by the colonists to fight a delaying action. It had been decided that the Americans would not fire unless the British did. The Americans waited. The Redcoats advanced.

Suddenly, a British rifle cracked. Ralph Waldo Emerson, a great American poet, described that scene in these stirring lines.

> *By the rude bridge that arched the flood,*
> *Their flag to April's breeze unfurled;*
> *Here once the embattled farmers stood,*
> *And fired the shot heard round the world!*

That shot "heard round the world" began the American Revolution.

Dead and wounded lay on the road. The British marched over the fallen, confident they would encounter little resistance at Concord.

But a surprise awaited them. Because Paul Revere had alerted the Americans, a large force had assembled. The gaudy uniforms of the British made excellent targets in the moonlight. After only a few exchanges, the Redcoats broke ranks and fled. Snipers shot at them from trees and attic windows. Concord was saved!

Thus began the war for independence of the American Colonies.

Paul Revere's memorable ride has been immortalized in the famous lines of Henry Wadsworth Longfellow:

> *Listen, my children, and you shall hear*
> *Of the midnight ride of Paul Revere,*
> *On the eighteenth of April, in Seventy-five;*
> *Hardly a man is now alive*
> *Who remembers that famous day and year.*
>
> *He said to his friend, "If the British march*
> *By land or sea from the town tonight,*
> *Hang a lantern aloft in the belfry arch*
> *Of the North Church tower as a signal light—*
> *One, if by land; and two, if by sea;*
> *And I on the opposite shore will be,*
> *Ready to ride and spread the alarm*
> *Through every Middlesex village and farm,*
> *For the country folk to be up and to arm."*
>
> *Then he said, "Good night!" and with muffled*
>   *oar*
> *Silently rowed to the Charlestown shore,*
> *Just as the moon rose over the bay,*
> *Where swinging wide at her moorings lay*
> *The Somerset, British man-of-war;*

A phantom ship, with each mast and spar
Across the moon like a prison bar,
And a huge black hulk, that was magnified
By its own reflection in the tide.

Meanwhile, his friend, through alley and street,
Wanders and watches with eager ears,
Till in the silence around him he hears
The muster of men at the barrack door,
The sound of arms, and the tramp of feet,
And the measured tread of the grenadiers,
Marching down to their boats on the shore.

Then he climbed the tower of the Old North
    Church,
By the wooden stairs, with stealthy tread,
To the belfry-chamber overhead;
And startled the pigeons from their perch
On the somber rafters, that round him made
Masses and moving shapes of shade—
By the trembling ladder, steep and tall,
To the highest window in the wall,
Where he paused to listen and look down
A moment on the roofs of the town,
And the moonlight flowing over all.

Meanwhile, impatient to mount and ride,
Booted and spurred, with a heavy stride
On the opposite shore walked Paul Revere.
Now he patted his horse's side,

Now gazed at the landscape far and near;
Then, impetuous, stamped the earth,
And turned and tightened his saddle-girth;
But mostly he watched with eager search
The belfry-tower of the Old North Church,
As it rose above the graves on the hill,
Lonely and spectral and somber and still.
And lo! as he looks, on the belfry's height
A glimmer, and then a gleam of light!
He springs to the saddle, the bridle he turns,
But lingers and gazes, till full on his sight
A second lamp in the belfry burns!

A hurry of hoofs in a village street,
A shape in the moonlight, a bulk in the dark,
And beneath, from the pebbles, in passing, a
    spark
Struck out by a steed flying fearless and fleet,
That was all! And yet, through the gloom and
    the light
The fate of a nation was riding that night;
And the spark struck out by that steed in his
    flight,
Kindled the land into flame with its heat.

It was twelve by the village clock
When he crossed the bridge into Medford town.
He heard the crowing of the cock,
And the barking of the farmer's dog,

And felt the damp of the river fog,
That rises after the sun goes down.

It was one by the village clock,
When he galloped into Lexington.
He saw the gilded weathercock
Swim in the moonlight as he passed,
And the meeting-house windows, blank and
    bare,
Gaze at him with a spectral glare,
As if they already stood aghast
At the bloody work they would look upon.

It was two by the village clock,
When he came to the bridge in Concord town.
He heard the bleating of the flock,
And the twitter of birds among the trees,
And felt the breath of the morning breeze
Blowing over the meadows brown.
And one was safe and asleep in his bed
Who at the bridge would be first to fall,
Who that day would be lying dead,
Pierced by a British musket-ball.

You know the rest. In the books you have read,
How the British Regulars fired and fled—
How the farmers gave them ball for ball,
From behind each fence and farmyard wall,
Chasing the redcoats down the lane,
Then crossing the fields to emerge again

Under the trees at the turn of the road,
And only pausing to fire and load.
So through the night rode Paul Revere;
And so through the night went his cry of alarm
To every Middlesex village and farm—
A cry of defiance, and not of fear,
A voice in the darkness, a knock at the door,
And a word that shall echo forevermore!
For borne on the night-wind of the Past,
Through all our history, to the last,
In the hour of darkness and peril and need,
The people will waken and listen to hear
The hurrying hoofbeats of that steed,
And the midnight message of Paul Revere.

GEORGE WASHINGTON
Father of his Country

On Christmas Eve, 1776, things looked very dark for the ragged little American Revolutionary Army. The brave farmers and townspeople who had volunteered to fight for their country's freedom were untrained and few in number. With only tattered clothing to protect them against the cruel cold of winter, little to eat, and little ammunition, they had fought a courageous but unequal battle against the well-armed, well-trained, well-fed British army. Greatly outnumbered, General George Washington's men had been forced to retreat from New York City into New Jersey. They had been pushed back still further, across the Delaware River, giving up half of the state of New Jersey!

Now they were camped on the far shore of the Delaware, trying to regain their strength, to stiffen their defenses against a new attack by the British. For the Americans knew that as soon as it grew cold enough for the river to freeze solid, Howe, the British General, would cross the ice and attack them. The only reason Howe was waiting for the river to freeze instead of crossing immediately by boat was that it was simpler to march his men across the ice; and he felt he could easily afford to take his time about attacking. He knew that Washington's army was unwilling to retreat further—and unable to advance. The American troops could only stay where they were, getting weaker and weaker all the time, until he swept down on them, swallowing them up in one gulp, like a bird of prey!

And Howe was not far from wrong. Washington's predicament was indeed almost hopeless. As a matter of fact, it was even worse than Howe probably guessed. For small and feeble as Washington's army now was, it was, at least, an army. In less than a week, however, Washington would have no army at all! His men had enlisted for only one year, and on New Year's day that year would be up. Discouraged by long months of defeat and lack of supplies, convinced that the war was already lost for the Americans, Washington's soldiers were preparing to leave the army as soon as their term of duty was up and return to their farms and families.

All in all, the situation was nearly as bad as could be

imagined. There was only one thing that saved the American army: the brains and persistence of its general, George Washington. Most other commanders would have thought of surrendering, of retreating, or at best, of strengthening their defenses and waiting to be attacked. But Washington thought of a clever, daring plan of offense, a plan that was to save the American army from almost certain defeat.

He knew that on the other side of the river, in the town of Trenton, the British—and the German troops they had hired to fight for them, the Hessians—were gayly preparing for their Christmas celebration, certain they had nothing to fear from the American army

*...Washington thought of a clever, daring
plan of offense ...*

across the river. Washington's plan was to cross the Delaware River on Christmas Night and take the English and Hessian soldiers by surprise. He knew they would be full of food, and drunk on wine from their Christmas dinner. He knew that the attack would be so unexpected that even though the American army was weaker, it would win! The last thing in the world General Howe expected Washington to do was attack, and the last time in the world he would have expected an attack was on Christmas Night. It was a very daring plan, indeed!

Picture a small band of American soldiers, huddled together on the shore of the river in the black of night, protected against the icy wind only by the thinnest of threadbare garments, waiting to get into the boats that would carry them across the inky waters, to victory— or to death! They knew that if their plan were discovered they all would be killed. They held their breaths while, with muffled oars, the boatsmen rowed them across the river.

A thin sheet of ice was beginning to cover the water. Perhaps someone on the enemy shore could hear the ice breaking as the oars dipped in and out. Perhaps their plan was already known, and the British were waiting for them on the opposite shore, ready to strike as soon as they had all landed! But whatever was in their hearts and minds, all night long the ragged ranks of Americans continued to march through the snow down to the shore of the Delaware, get into boats, and row across the river.

At dawn, they attacked.

The Hessians, drunk and half-asleep after a night of wild parties, hardly realized what was happening to them. In half an hour the fighting was over, and the English had surrendered Trenton to Washington.

In the American army's darkest hour, George Washington's brilliant plan had saved the day! When his soldiers' term of enlistment was up, they were no longer discouraged and they volunteered to fight on. The American Congress, which had become convinced that the cause was lost, suddenly saw that it was still possible for the Revolutionary forces to win, and it obtained large amounts of money with which to buy equipment and pay the soldiers. The British, dismayed at the courage and strength of the Americans, abandoned the idea of capturing Philadelphia that winter. This put the Americans in a much better military position than any one had ever dreamed possible—all thanks to General George Washington.

But the man who led his country to victory against one of the most powerful nations in the world was more than a great soldier. He was also a great statesman, elected to be the first President of the United States. George Washington is always spoken of as: "First in war, first in peace, and first in the hearts of his countrymen."

THOMAS PAINE
Phamphleteer of the Revolution

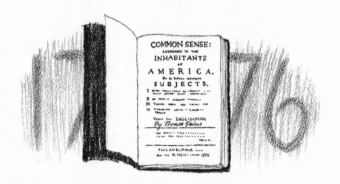

In the freezing December night, groups of soldiers stood along the Delaware River, listening to these soaring words: "These are the times that try men's souls! The summer soldier and sunshine patriot will, in this crisis, shrink from the service of their country. Tyranny, like hell, is not easily conquered!"

General George Washington listened, too. Although he had read Tom Paine's pamphlet, the words, spoken aloud by their author, moved him all over again. On the faces of the soldiers nearest him, Washington could see rapt concentration. The men seemed to have forgotten their cold and misery, stirred as they were by Paine's ringing words.

Soon Washington ordered his men to row across the

river in the blackness of the night and attack the British and the Hessian mercenaries in Trenton. The first offensive of the Revolutionary War was triumphant.

That night Thomas Paine, foot soldier in the American Revolutionary Army, and author of the pamphlet *Crisis,* lay awake.

Memory followed memory, as Tom went back to his own beginnings. He was born in Thetford, England. His Quaker father, a corset maker, had difficulty providing for his family. When Tom wanted to go to sea, his father refused permission. Instead, Tom was obliged to attend grammar school.

After school hours, Tom worked beside his father taking measurements for ladies' corsets and bodices, but he detested the work.

At eighteen, he ran away to sea. When the voyage was over, Tom went to London. Here the libraries and museums fascinated him; and he spent considerable time studying mathematics, philosophy, and astronomy.

But misfortune dogged him. His wife died in childbirth, and his poverty forced him to work again as a corset maker.

Some time later, he found a job as a tax collector. But in this job he was expected to wink at law evasion and to accept bribes. He was repelled by the corruption, had a falling out with his his superior, and was discharged.

For a time, he took any odd job that was available.

Then he succeeded in once again getting a job as a tax collector. But life was a continual struggle against poverty. Books were as necessary to Thomas Paine as food, and often he went without food to buy books.

One day, his fellow workers persuaded Tom to petition Parliament for higher wages on their behalf. He did so. As a result, he lost his job again.

So it was that in 1774, alone and poor, Tom Paine thought of going to America. The only American he knew was Benjamin Franklin with whom he had corresponded on matters relating to electricity. When Franklin came to London on a diplomatic mission for the American government, he and Paine got together. After talking with Franklin, Tom made up his mind.

With a letter of introduction to Franklin's son-in-law in Philadelphia, Paine left for the New World. Soon after his arrival, Paine became a contributing editor on the *Pennsylvania Magazine.*

In 1776, there appeared a startling pamphlet called *Common Sense.* It was written by Tom Paine. The journalist demanded America's independence from England and stressed the establishment of a strong federal union. Soon *Common Sense* became the champion of liberty, winning the approval of George Washington and Thomas Jefferson.

In 1776, Paine joined Washington's army, and suffered hunger and cold along with the other soldiers. During this period, Paine wrote articles about the war

THOMAS PAINE 63

which came to be known as the *Crisis* articles. Washington asked Paine to read aloud the first of these essays to the bedraggled small army. It was this first *Crisis* article which fired the spirit of the American soldiers and sent them across the Delaware to win the battle of Trenton.

In 1777, Paine was made Secretary to the Congressional Committee of Foreign Affairs. But his uncompromising honesty brought him into trouble. He exposed the American ambassador to France in an unfavorable light, and thereby incurred the anger of some important political figures. Paine was forced to resign.

Once again Paine endured poverty. Then, fortunately, he was appointed Clerk of the Pennsylvania Assembly. During this time, he gave freely of his salary to the Revolutionary cause, and he continued to write his *Crisis* pamphlets without financial recompense.

In 1883, the war for independence ended. Tom Paine wrote his last *Crisis* pamphlet. All over America men read these words: "The times that tried men's souls are over; and the greatest and completest revolution the world ever knew gloriously and happily accomplished. It was the cause of America that made me an author. The force with which it struck my mind, and the dangerous condition the country appeared to me to be in, made it impossible for me, feeling as I did, to be silent."

After the Revolution, the enemies Paine had made by his outspokenness continued to harass him. Only at the repeated urging of George Washington did Thomas

Washington asked Paine to read aloud the first of these essays to the bedraggled small army.

Paine receive a house and farm from the New York Legislature, and a pension from the state of Pennsylvania. Finally, Congress voted him $3,000.

With independence, there now seemed no need for Tom Paine's pen. But the man was still intellectually active. He worked out a plan for the building of an iron bridge, superior to the wooden ones in existence at the time. In 1787, he went to France and then to England to seek funds so that his bridge could be built. But world events were to interfere with his plans.

France stood on the threshold of a revolution. As Tom Paine had sympathized with the Americans, so did he sympathize with the French. In England, he published an essay which he called *Rights of Man*. Unexpectedly, Paine found his work suppressed by the British Prime Minister, and Paine learned with alarm that he was to be tried for treason.

Paine fled to France. At first, the ardent revolutionaries treated Paine as a friend and he was made a member of the French Assembly. But as the revolution continued and the Reign of Terror began, the blood shed by the people he wanted to help, revolted Paine. As was his custom, he spoke out strongly. He was removed from his position and cast into jail.

During the excesses of the revolution, Paine continued writing. Just before he went to jail, he completed the *Age of Reason*. In this book, he boldly stated his views on organized religion. "I believe in one God and no more," he wrote, "and I hope for happiness beyond this life," he insisted, but this statement couldn't save him. When publication in London and Paris brought his unorthodox attitudes to the attention of the public, Paine was falsely denounced as an atheist. Behind the bars of his prison, Tom Paine knew nothing of the controversy he had raised. Alone and desolate, despair overwhelmed him.

A group of Americans in Paris tried to secure Paine's release, but American government officials decided not to interfere. They agreed that governmental intercession might provoke the fiery young French Republic to condemn Paine to death.

When James Monroe arrived as America's Minister to France, he was horrified to learn that Paine was still imprisoned. Though he arranged immediately for his release, Paine came out of his confinement a sick and bitter man. His old friend Thomas Jefferson, then President of the United States, arranged for his safe passage back to America.

In the country he had once so deeply inspired, his enemies continued their slander, and his last years were plagued by poverty and illness. Because Paine was reviled for his religious views, the tendency has been to overlook the part played in the struggle for American freedom. Today's historians have begun to pay him homage; and today, Thomas Paine is revered as a great American patriot.

THOMAS JEFFERSON
Champion of Democracy

"I think I love this place better than any place in the world," said Tom Jefferson. He sat up suddenly. "When I grow up, I'll build a house right here, and live on my mountain for the rest of my life."

Dabney laughed. "I believe you really mean it. But it won't be easy, Tom, dragging materials all the way up here."

Tom's red hair gleamed in the sun. He was fourteen, about the same age as his friend, Dabney Carr. The boys had harnessed their horses to a tree. In the distance stretched the great forests of the Piedmont; with their young, sharp eyes, on a clear day they could see all the way to the distant Blue Ridge.

In answer to Dabney's objection about the formidable task involved, Tom said, "I don't care, I'll work it out somehow."

And he did. Years later, on that same mountain, Thomas Jefferson drew up his own architectural plans and built a beautiful and gracious house which he called Monticello.

Almost from his very beginning as a lad, Jefferson showed those qualities of determination and fortitude which were to make him become one of the greatest statesmen the United States has ever known.

He was born at Shadwell in Albemarle County of Virginia. He grew up on the frontier. His father was a farmer and a surveyor, and the Jefferson family was counted among the first families of Virginia.

Tom spent his days hunting, fishing and riding, but his life did not altogether consist of play. He began his studies at the age of five; and later he learned Latin, Greek, and French. He was sent to Latin School, one of the best in the colony. Upon graduation, he entered William and Mary College, in Williamsburg, where he studied law.

At twenty-four, Tom stood a big, strapping red-head over six feet tall. He was admitted to the bar. From then on, public service was to engage the greater part of his life. Although he was a landed proprietor and a slaveowner, he never concurred in the aristocratic point of view. In fact, it annoyed him to be called an aristocrat. Even as a young man he became a champion of human rights, and it is in this role that Thomas Jefferson stands as one of the great figures of all time.

While Monticello, his dream home on top of his beloved mountain was being built, Tom involved himself with law, farming, scientific, and literary projects. He loved music, and in the evenings he played his violin while Martha, his wife, accompanied him on the harpsichord. Jefferson lived the life of a gentleman farmer. He spent those early days improving his large estates, working on legal matters, and collecting a library which later was to serve as the foundation for the Library of Congress.

In 1769, Jefferson became a member of the Virginia legislative body known as the House of Burgesses. There he met Patrick Henry. Jefferson quickly allied himself to this ardent liberal. In those pre-Revolutionary days, the American colonies were groaning under grievances inflicted by the mother country, England. As a protest against the English Tea Act of 1773, the colonists in Boston dumped a whole ship-load of tea into the Boston harbor. Reprisals were bound to take place.

Jefferson and his liberal friends decided to make Boston's cause the cause of Virginia. "I propose," said Thomas Jefferson to the Assembly, "that Virginia mark June 1st as a fast day. This will show Boston that it does not stand alone." This dramatic gesture was observed throughout Virginia. The irate British governor dissolved the Assembly and forced the colonials to form a group of their own.

In 1774, Jefferson drew up his "Summary View of the Rights of British America." In this document, he stated that the English Parliament had no control over the American colonies; that allegiance was owed only to the English king; that tyrannical acts by the sovereign could force the colonists to renounce allegiance to the crown. King George III angrily thundered that the Americans must be beaten into submission.

A second Continental Congress was held. Jefferson took a leading part. He drafted two historical documents: "A Declaration of Causes" and "Necessity of Taking Up Arms."

During the spring of 1776, the clamor for colonial independence reached new heights. In response, Congress appointed a committee to draw up a declaration of independence from England. Thomas Jefferson was asked to prepare the draft. The words he wrote became immortal, a statement of the basic philosophy of the American people:

> *When in the Course of human events, it becomes necessary for one people to dissolve the political bands that have connected them with another, and to assume*

*among the powers of the earth,
the separate and equal station to
which the Laws of Nature and of
Nature's God entitle them, a decent respect to the opinions
of mankind requires that they
should declare the causes which
impel them to the separation.*

*We hold these truths to be
self-evident: that all men are created equal; that they are en-
dowed by their Creator with certain unalienable Rights; that
among these are Life, Liberty and
the pursuit of Happiness.*

It is on these ringing words that the foundations of
American liberty stand.

After serving two terms as Governor of the State of
Virginia, Jefferson was stunned and shaken by the
death of his beloved wife, Martha. He expressed the
desire to give up public life; he wanted to devote himself solely to his young daughters. But this was not his
destiny.

In 1783, he was elected to Congress. During his
term, he worked out a decimal system of currency and
secured its adoption.

Roughly two years later, Jefferson was appointed by

the United States Government as Minister to France.
George Washington, the first President of the United
States, called upon him to join his cabinet as Secretary
of State. In the government, Jefferson led the Democratic forces, combating the Federalists, who under Alexander Hamilton, favored the privileged few.

*Congress appointed a committee to draw up a
declaration of independence.*

In 1800, Jefferson, after having served a term as Vice President, was elected President of the United States. One of the greatest achievements of his administration was the negotiation of the Louisiana Purchase, the acquisition of that vast territory which lies between the Mississippi River and the Rocky Mountains.

At sixty-five, having served a second term of office in the Presidency, Thomas Jefferson retired. Now, finally, there was time to do what he wished: to experiment

with new crops and techniques of farming, to improve his flower and herb gardens, to indulge his love of music and study.

For many years, Jefferson had been giving thought to building a university. Ideally, this university would advocate freedom—freedom of the human mind to explore every subject susceptible to human contemplation. Out of this dream he created the beautiful and progressive University of Virginia.

After his retirement, a steady stream of visitors came to Monticello, both to visit the great man and to view the many inventions and innovations he had originated. On the porch ceiling they caught glimpses of a weathervane with a dial. Here, too, they saw the first storm windows, a revolving writing chair, a dumbwaiter, an elevator, a movable bed on pulleys, and many other evidences of Jefferson's scientific inventiveness.

Fifty years, exactly to the day, after the Declaration of Independence was adopted, Thomas Jefferson died.

Many of the liberal reforms that Jefferson urged and fought for could not bring to fruition within his lifetime. He fought slavery, but in those days, he could make no change in that institution. Nor could he provide public education for everyone who sought it. But Thomas Jefferson did bring his countrymen a law providing for religious freedom, a set of Constitutional amendments which provided for civil rights. His was a legacy of democratic freedom.

NATHAN HALE
Martyr of the American Revolution

During the American Revolution, in a little town in Connecticut, there lived a young man whose name was Nathan Hale. He was one of the first to join the American Army. He was a good soldier, and soon he was made a captain.

The war was going badly for the Americans. Nathan Hale heard that someone was needed to go behind the British lines to get some information. He volunteered to be the American spy.

He disguised himself as a Dutch schoolteacher. He was discovered and captured by the British. Nathan Hale had known before he had volunteered, how dangerous it was to be a spy. And he knew, now that he was captured, what his fate was to be. He knew he

75

"I only regret that I have but one life to lose for my country!"

would be hanged.

Nathan Hale was not even twenty-one years old. After his sentence was pronounced, he declared, "I only regret that I have but one life to lose for my country!" These words became an immortal legacy to the cause of freedom.

JOHN PAUL JONES
Founder of the American Navy

"I will have nothing to do with ships which do not sail fast, for I intend to go in harm's way." So wrote the young sea-captain John Paul Jones, asking for a fleet to fight the British Navy.

During the American Revolutionary War, the English did not hesitate to land their warships along the American coast and burn and destroy helpless American towns. Young Paul Jones, who had been at sea since he was a boy of twelve, believed that with courage and bold fighting the American Navy, small and weak as it was, could fight successfully against the mighty British fleet.

The British had hundreds of warships and merchant ships. They were the undisputed rulers of the seas.

But Paul Jones didn't just talk bravely. He begged
for a chance to prove that he could do what he said.
He was given the command of a small sailing vessel
called the *Ranger*. In those days all ships were sailing
ships, for the steamship had not been invented as yet.
Jones set out across the Atlantic. As he drew near England, he met a British merchant ship, attacked it, took
everything of value, and sent the captured vessel into
a French port. "Now," he announced, "we sail for
England!"

"What! How can we dare to approach the English
coast?" cried his First Lieutenant.

"We will not only approach the English coast," declared Paul Jones, "we will raid it as they have raided
ours." As he spoke, the coast of England came into
sight. There lay the port of Whitehaven, with many
British ships tied up at its docks.

As night fell, Jones gave the order to put out the
longboats. Some of his crew were so frightened they
were on the verge of mutiny. But Captain Jones commanded them to move fast.

Silently, they rowed into the port. The town was
sleeping peacefully. Danger seemed so far away to the
English that even the sentries were asleep! One by
one, Captain Jones and his men bound and gagged the
British guards. In a few minutes, without firing a shot,
John Paul Jones and his men had captured the main
fort guarding the bay at Whitehaven. Then they si-

lently rowed across the harbor and set fire to the ships tied up there.

As the sky lit up with the flames, the amazed English rushed from their homes to see the American captain return to his ship. Morning came and Jones and his men were sinking into slumber when the watch reported the approach of a large warship.

The men were terrified. They knew the British man-of-war must have found out that they had just burned the harbor of Whitehaven. The crew begged Jones to flee. But Paul Jones was undismayed.

The fight began. The British warship, the *Drake,* was indeed much bigger than the *Ranger,* and had many more guns on its decks. But the *Ranger* had Captain John Paul Jones. He skillfully sailed his ship close past the bow of the *Drake* in such a way that the British guns could not point at the *Ranger.* The commander of the *Drake* was baffled by such daring. The *Ranger* twisted and turned so that it could fire on the English ship and it fired so that every shot counted.

When the battle ended, John Paul Jones' little ship was badly battered. Its decks were covered with wounded. But his proud sailors watched the flag of the British warship lowered in defeat.

For months after this glorious victory, Jones was praised and cheered by his countrymen. He was promised a fleet again and again, but delay followed delay. He could not bear inaction. Rather than wait any longer, he took command of an old clumsy ship named the *Bon Homme Richard*. Actually he was supposed to have been given command of six more ships. But when the other captains heard that he planned to sail near the coast of England and Scotland, four of them refused to follow him. So Jones set out with the *Bon Homme Richard,* accompanied by two other vessels.

Within six weeks, John Paul Jones, now a Commodore in the American Navy, sank over twenty British merchant ships! He spread such fears throughout the British Isles that English ships hardly dared to leave their ports. Finally, with their holds packed with British prisoners, the three American ships set sail for a spot in the North Sea where Jones knew that a large fleet of British merchantmen were expected to pass. He knew, too, that the English merchant fleet would be protected by British warships. But Paul Jones felt that this was his big chance.

The story of that battle has made the name of John Paul Jones immortal. In the moonlight, the *Bon Homme Richard* was attacked by the British warship *Serapis,* a great, new, powerful ship with two rows of large cannon—more than twice as many as the American man-of-war.

Almost any other man would have given up. During the long and bloody fight, Jones saw his men falling on all sides. The decks were stained with blood! The sea was pouring in through the many holes made by the enemy's cannon balls. Finally, the captain of the *Serapis* called out to the damaged vessel, "Do you surrender?" But the dauntless Jones, in a voice of thunder, shouted, "Never! I have just begun to fight!"

To keep his helpless ship from floating away, Jones tied it to the *Serapis!* The battle turned into a hand-to-hand fight. Suddenly came the cry, "The ship is sinking!"

The English prisoners who had escaped from the hold were desperate with fear. They were about to attack Jones. But the American turned on them and shouted, "The *Serapis* is sinking, too. If you want to save your lives, man the pumps!"

"Do you surrender?"

So the desperate prisoners, instead of attacking Jones, rushed to the pumps to keep the ship afloat. And Jones, with the handful of his men still alive, turned on the crew of the *Serapis*.

Up till the last moment, it seemed all would be lost. But Jones was undismayed. He fought on when all hope seemed gone, and in the end the *Bon Homme Richard* conquered—a glorious victory for the Americans.

Small wonder, then, that John Paul Jones is considered the founder of the American Navy—a navy that will never forget him.

"Never! I have just begun to fight!"

DANIEL BOONE
Intrepid Frontiersman

When the white man first discovered America, it was inhabited by Indians. The new settlers had to build stockades, or forts, for protection against the savages. These stockades were made of heavy logs set closely together and driven into the ground to form a high wall. A big gate cut in the stockade was kept bolted tight. Women and children were seldom allowed to go outside the enclosure, and only the bravest men ventured into the forest to hunt animals.

In the year 1770, Daniel Boone, a famous woodsman, lived in one of these frontier settlements. Located in Kentucky, it was named Boonesborough, after him.

One cold winter day, Boone came rushing into the stockade. "Someone has killed the Indian chief, King

Cornstalk!" he shouted. "The Shawnees are on the warpath. No one must leave the stockade!"

The settlers always obeyed Boone. He knew more about Indians than anyone else in America. When only a boy, he had made friends with the redskins and he had learned all the secrets of the forest. He knew how the Indians felt towards the settlers who had invaded their lands. He knew how fierce they could be. They would yell and whoop, and charge down on a stockade to massacre all the inhabitants. The Indians would then hang the scalps of their victims on their belts and brag about the number of white men they had killed.

A few weeks later, Boonesborough ran out of salt. In those pioneer days, salt was very important. Salt was used to preserve meats and hides. That was the only way meat could be saved for winter food. Now, in spite of the danger, Boone had to assemble thirty men to go on a salt expedition. When the party arrived at the salt lick, they set up camp. They filled big kettles with water from the salt springs. Then they built fires under the kettles, boiling the water until only the salt was left.

Boone went out hunting to provide the camp with meat. He shot a buffalo, cleaned and skinned it with his hunting knife, and then lashed the carcass to his saddle with thongs of hide. He was leading his horse back to camp when suddenly a fierce snowstorm blew up. The wind howled. Snow swirled around Boone, nearly blinding him. He could hardly see a foot ahead; and of course he couldn't know that he was being followed by Indians. Usually he could detect the slightest sound in the forest; but now the wind shrieked so that even Boone could not hear the Indians approaching.

Cautiously, six Indians drew very close, and then rushed upon him. Quick as a flash, Boone reached for his hunting knife. He tried to slash the thongs that tied the buffalo to his horse, so that he could gallop away. But the knife was frozen fast in its sheath, and Boone was captured.

The Indians were very proud when they discovered their captive was the famous Daniel Boone. They watched his every move. They had heard that once before Boone had escaped from the Indians by jumping over a cliff and landing on some trees sixty feet below! He wouldn't escape now! When Boone reached the Indian camp, he found a tremendous fire thirty feet long blazing to the skies. Around the huge fire sat scores of ferocious Shawnee warriors wearing warpaint! Obviously, they were set to attack Boonesborough! With so many of its fighting men at the salt lick, Boonesborough wouldn't stand a chance.

Then the warriors took Daniel Boone to Chief Blackfish. Boone told the Chief that if he spared the settlement, Boone would lead the Shawnees to his fighting men and persuade them to surrender to the Indians.

"Promise me you will not torture my men!" said Boone.

Chief Blackfish agreed.

Next morning, Boone led a hundred and twenty warriors to the salt lick. The white men jumped for their guns. "Don't fire!" Boone yelled. "If you do, you will be massacred!"

The men stood in a circle and stacked their rifles on the ground as Boone told them to do. But despite the promise of Chief Blackfish, many of the savages wanted to execute all the prisoners anyhow. Boone made a long speech to the Indians. "These men have done you no harm," he reminded them. When he finished speaking, the Indians took a vote amongst themselves by passing a war-club. Fifty-nine warriors dashed it to the ground to signify that the men should be killed; but sixty-one let the club pass by. The men were saved by only two votes!

Back at camp, the warriors began clearing a path through the snow. They were preparing *the gauntlet,* and told Boone this was something special reserved for him. Two rows of Indians would stand facing each other. Boone was to run between the rows, and Indians would strike at him with spears and tomahawks. Usually, a captive was cut to ribbons as he ran the gauntlet and hardly anyone ever got through alive.

But Boone knew the ways of the Indians and had figured out just how to handle himself in such a situation. He ran head on into the very first Indian, bowled him over, and grabbed his shield. Then, at full speed, he dashed zig-zag through the rows using the shield to parry most of the blows. The sharp tomahawks spun around him, but he somehow managed to get past the two murderous rows, wounded but not seriously hurt.

Chief Blackfish was so impressed with Boone's courage and skill that he decided to adopt him as his own son. Of course, for this great honor Boone had to be especially prepared. All his hair except for a small tuft on the top of his head was plucked from his scalp. It was dreadfully painful. But Boone dared not show how he suffered, else he might be executed as unworthy of being the son of the chief. Now the whole tribe treated him with more respect than ever.

Days passed, and Boone, pretending to be happy, bided his time. When summer came, the Indians once again began to mix their warpaints, and Boone surmised they were again planning to attack Boonesborough.

Indians from other tribes joined the camp until there were some five hundred warriors. The settlement had to be warned or everyone in Boonesborough would be massacred. But Boone himself was guarded very closely.

One day, some Indians went out on a hunting party to shoot wild turkeys in the forest. The shooting made much noise, and Boone was alert to every opportunity.

Knowing the redskins wouldn't hear him, he raced
swiftly away on his horse while the warriors weren't
looking. But some squaws saw him as he galloped out
of camp and soon the Indians were hot on his trail.
Boone rode his horse down a shallow stream to make it
impossible for the Indians to follow his trail. Then
Boone let his horse loose and continued into the forest
on foot, running along fallen trees to hide his tracks.
He covered the one hundred and sixty miles to Boonesborough in four days! This exploit has gone down in
history as one of the greatest feats of endurance ever
recorded.

When Boone arrived at the settlement, he immediately set out to repair the stockade and prepare the fort
for the Shawnee attack. The defenders were few, indeed. Word was sent to the other frontier settlements
to send as many men as could be spared. The Indians
were so numerous it was certain they meant to capture
Boonesborough and then go on to take every settlement in Kentucky!

Men came from near and far to hold the fort. For a
long time, all was quiet. Then the Indians finally approached with the white flag of truce.

Boone went outside the stockade with a few other
men. Chief Blackfish spread out a panther-skin for a
peace talk. When Boone refused to surrender the settlement, the Indians pretended they wanted to shake
hands in friendship. But when they took hold of the

settlers' hands, they jerked their arms, pulled the settlers off balance, and started to drag them away.

Boone made a mighty lunge and Chief Blackfish,
who had grasped Boone's hand, went tumbling on his
back! The other men managed to break loose and
dashed for the stockade. Hundreds of Indians concealed in the bushes let out blood-chilling war whoops
as they charged the settlement. Boone waved his hat
wildly as a signal to the fort to start firing. Bullets
whizzed past him and his men as they raced to the fort.
They slammed the stockade gate shut, just in time!

For many days and nights the fight went on, the
longest Indian raid on record in Kentucky! Fifty men

*Boone waved his hat wildly as a signal to the fort
to start firing.*

were inside the fort and five hundred Indians outside! Again and again, the cabins inside the stockade caught fire from the Shawnees' flaming arrows.

After days of fighting, suddenly the firing stopped. Here was something strange indeed! A queer noise was heard and soon Boone learned that the Indians were tunneling underground to blow up the stockade with gunpowder. This was something that even Daniel Boone couldn't cope with. Any moment, the men expected to hear the tunnel explode. The Indians would be on them, shrieking and brandishing their tomahawks. The settlers were miserable, hungry, and exhausted. It rained steadily and that made them feel worse.

But in the morning all was quiet! A kind of miracle had taken place! The rain had soaked the gunpowder and ruined it. What's more, the tunnel had caved in because the earth was softened by the rain.

The discouraged Indians left, never to return! The rejoicing of the settlers was unbounded!

Soon, covered wagons began to roll through the forests of Kentucky.

To this day, there stands a monument in tribute to the stalwart and intrepid frontiersman, Daniel Boone. His valiant defense against the Shawnees saved the settlements of Kentucky and opened up the Midwest to the pioneers.

LEWIS AND CLARK
Explorers of the West

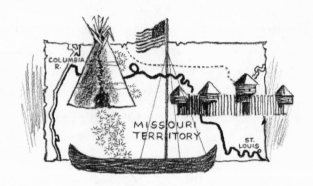

In 1803, under President Thomas Jefferson, the great Louisiana Purchase had been negotiated. The United States had bought half a continent, a vast tract of unknown land. Here were mountains, streams, and deserts—a whole new world.

Meriwether Lewis, private secretary to the President, had requested Jefferson to let him lead an expedition through the new territory. Jefferson agreed, and Congress appropriated funds for the first exploration of the West by a white man.

Lewis was excited. It was an adventure he had sought and dreamed about for a long time. Plans were developing. The President spoke to Lewis about a co-leader for the expedition.

"The man I have in mind," said Jefferson, "is a fellow Virginian and an Army officer. His name is William Clark."

Lewis was delighted. He knew Clark. He and Clark had fought in the Indian wars together.

The expedition planned to go as far as possible up the Missouri River to make surveys and scientific observations. Reports would be rendered about the Indian tribes in the territory, and data would be taken on the plant and animal life of the vast unknown region.

It took months to choose men, select equipment, ready the boats, and purchase materials with which to trade with the Indians.

In May, 1804, near what was the small trading settlement of St. Louis, the expedition started out. Lewis and Clark were supported by 27 soldiers and two interpreters. A dozen more men would accompany the party as far as the present site of Bismarck, North Dakota.

Three boats had been especially built to navigate the Missouri River. Of these, two were open. The third was a flat-bottom boat over 50 feet long on which was mounted an iron gun on a swivel. This boat had 22 oars and a great square sail. From its mast flew the American flag.

On board there was a motley assortment of tools and trinkets—beads, brooches, rings, calico shirts, bells, kettles, needles, cloth, and medals for the Indian chiefs and their cohorts. On each medal there was engraved a picture of the Great White Chief in Washington, President Thomas Jefferson. And then, of course, there were hoards of rations: soup stock, flour, tea, cornmeal, salt, and pepper.

The expedition traveled 12 to 15 miles each day. The explorers took all summer to reach North Dakota, the land of the Mandam Indians. The red men here were friendly; game was plentiful; and Lewis and Clark decided to camp in this locality until spring. They built a fort, and searched the woods for species of animal and plant life.

Then one snowy day, a fur trapper appeared at the fort and asked to speak to the leader. The stranger was dark and bearded, and spoke with a French accent. With him there was a black-haired young Indian girl.

The trapper, a French-Canadian by the name of Charbonneau, introduced the Indian girl as his wife, Sacajawea.

"I have heard of your expedition," he said. "You will need a guide. I know this country well, but Sacajawea knows it like the palm of her hand."

The captains accepted his services. They agreed that Sacajawea would be helpful in conferring with the Indians; but how helpful she was to be, they couldn't possibly guess.

That spring, 16 men of the expedition returned to St. Louis with reports. An item in their journal reveals

that some of the articles they carried with them were "a stuffed male and female antelope with their skeletons; a weasel; three squirrels; the skeleton of a prairie wolf; a pair of large elk horns; a variety of animal skins; articles of Indian dress."

It was now April, 1805. The expedition set off again, this time to follow the Missouri River to its source. Since

. . . the river was too shallow for the 50-foot boat . . .

the river was too shallow for the 50-foot boat, they
were compelled to abandon it and divide its load between the two smaller craft. Much of the equipment,
including the swivel gun, was left behind.

One afternoon in May, Lewis climbed a steep slope
and saw in the distance mountain peaks which towered

higher than any he had ever seen. Here were the beau-
teous Rockies. But the appalling task of how to cross
this huge barrier on foot, with packs of supplies on the
backs of the men, would daunt any but the stoutest
spirit. No roads, no sources for food, no communica-
tion of any kind with anyone at all—this was the pros-
pect that faced them.

"We must buy pack horses from the Shoshone Indians," said Lewis.

They knew that this tribe was located somewhere in
the region. With four of his bravest men, Lewis set out
in this wilderness to find the Indians. After exhausting
climbs over steep mountains and with food almost gone,
Lewis finally located the Shoshones. Suspiciously, the
red men eyed the strangers who bore a red, white, and
blue banner.

Lewis slowly approached the chief. He was on foot.
The Indian towered above him, high on his horse. In
the few words Sacajawea had taught him, Lewis explained that he came in peace.

The chief threw down his spear and dismounted.
Lewis bargained with the Indians, offering fabulous
gifts in exchange for horses.

The next day the Shoshones accompanied Lewis to
the fort. Sacajawea had come out to greet the Indians.
Suddenly, she pointed to the chief and cried aloud.

Everyone stared at her. She uttered words none of the
expedition could understand. But the chief understood

and ran to embrace the girl who was none other than his very own sister, who had been stolen away from her tribe many years before.

Following this joyful reunion, the Indians became very friendly with the expedition, and agreed to sell the white men all the horses they needed. In addition, the Shoshones would provide a guide to lead the explorers across the mountains.

After many, many days of trudging through rain and snow under the hardest conditions imaginable, the Lewis and Clark Expedition finally reached the waters of the Columbia River. On November 7, 1805, Clark wrote in his journal, "Great joy in Camp. We are in view of the Ocean, this great Pacific Ocean which we have been so long anxious to see."

In the spring, Lewis and Clark were ready to return to St. Louis. By late summer, the expedition had returned to the lands of the Mandam, where they took leave of Charbonneau and Sacajawea.

On September 23, 1806, the expedition reached the starting point of St. Louis. Lewis and Clark had traversed 9,000 miles of wilderness!

In appreciation, a grateful Congress ceded grants of land to Meriwether Lewis and William Clark in 1807. It was through their grueling journey into the vast trackless territory beyond the Missouri River that the great West had been opened up to settlers. Many Americans would follow.

SAMUEL HOUSTON

Builder of Texan Independence

The pioneer woman was giving her order to the tall, lanky boy behind the counter. "I need five pounds of beans," she said, "and ten pounds of flour and . . . I'll want three lengths of this calico."

"Yes Ma'am," fifteen year old Sam Houston replied. He smothered a groan as he got her supplies together and cut the calico.

Shortly after the Houston family had moved from Virginia to Tennessee, Sam's mother became a part owner of a small trading store. Knowing how much Sam disliked farming, his mother had said to him, "Would you like to work in the store with your brothers?" The thought of being cooped up all day in a little shop did not appeal to Sam in the least, but maybe that was better than the dull lonely work of farming. "I guess I would," Sam had decided. But his work in the store became more and more boring.

A year or so earlier, Sam had become friendly with a Cherokee lad named John Rogers. Sam had visited the island where the Cherokees lived and had met the tribe. When the boring work in the store exasperated him, Sam often daydreamed of running off and living with the Indians.

And one day he did. He took a canoe and sailed to the island home of the Cherokees.

Chief Oolooteka greeted him warmly. "It gives me great pleasure to see you, my son," he said.

"I have come to stay," Sam said simply. "I would like to live among your people." It took some persuasion but the Chief finally gave his permission.

The tall young white man wore Indian clothes, and worked hard to learn the Cherokee language. Some time later, Chief Oolooteka said to him, "Your name among us is now Colloneh. It means *The Raven.*"

Gone now were the long days of confinement in the store. Sam learned to track deer in the forest, to snare rabbits, and to catch fish. He loved the evenings when he sat with the Indians in the council chamber and listened to the talk of the chieftains.

Sam Houston spent almost three years with the Cherokees—years that made a deep impression on him. Most important, Sam's feeling of respect for the Indians lasted throughout his life. He fought against injustice to the redman wherever he encountered it.

After leaving the Cherokees, Sam joined the U. S. Army, then engaged in war with the Creeks, who had vowed to kill or drive out every white settler in Alabama. In one battle, he was so severely wounded he was left on the battlefield and given up for dead. Only his will to live enabled him to recover.

When he left the army, Sam took up the study of law. He practiced his profession in Lebanon, Tennessee. His record as a war hero, combined with his ability to make friends, resulted in his election to Congress in 1823. Four years later, Sam Houston became Governor of Tennessee.

He resigned from the Governorship in 1829 and then moved west to become an Indian trader in Texas. His friend, Jim Bowie, had spoken to him many times of Texas. Bowie told Houston of the vastness of that territory, of its enormous plains, of the richness of the bottom lands along the rivers, and the plentifulness of game. And one fine day, Sam Houston packed up and moved to Texas.

During those days, Texas was owned by Mexico, and trouble had been growing between the American settlers and the Mexican Government. The Americans decided to request their independence from Mexico, and they sent Stephen Austin to negotiate. When word came that Austin had been put in prison for treason, the Texans reacted with fury. They asked Sam Houston to lead them in a war for independence.

Sam's experience warned him that the time was not yet ripe. "It would be foolhardy to push Texas into a bloody struggle with Mexico before we are fully prepared," he said emphatically. Nonetheless, the war began. The first shots of the Texas Revolution were fired at the town of Gonzales.

Sam Houston organized a Texan army and became its Commander-in-chief. Confident because of an easy victory at San Antonio, the American volunteers were certain that they could easily defeat the Mexicans. But Houston warned that the Mexican dictator, Santa Anna, would be a formidable enemy.

Not heeding his advice that the fortifications at San Antonio be destroyed and abandoned, Lt. Colonel William B. Travis and James Bowie took joint command of 187 men at San Antonio. On February 23, the dreaded Santa Anna appeared with a mighty army of more than 6,000 Mexicans.

Travis and Bowie moved their men into the Alamo Mission, answering the Mexican demand for surrender with a mighty cannon shot.

Houston and the other members of the newly formed Texas government received, at Washington-on-the-Brazos, by courier a desperate message from Travis saying, "I shall never surrender nor retreat . . . Victory or Death!"

Houston . . . rode his white horse to the front of his lines, raised his sword and began the advance.

It was then that Houston prepared to gather his 300 men at Gonzales and go to the aid of the Alamo defenders. Unknown to him, however, was the terrible fact that on the thirteenth day of battle, Santa Anna's fighters stormed the Alamo. The Americans fought valiantly, from building to building, room to room, desperately using even their rifles as clubs. The exhausted defenders were finally overcome and slaughtered.

Too late, a heartbroken Sam Houston heard the dreadful news.

Houston vowed that the Alamo would be avenged. He set about to develop an army of strong, well-disciplined fighters.

In April, 1836, at the Battle of San Jacinto, Sam

Houston kept his vow. Just before that battle, Houston said to his men, "Any man who is afraid does not have to cross the Bayou. But remember that any man who dies does so for a just and glorious cause. And remember the Alamo!"

The Mexican force was twice the size of the American force. Houston decided his best hope lay in a surprise attack. Feeling certain that Santa Anna expected a dawn offensive, Houston took him unawares with an attack at three thirty in the afternoon. The American general rode his white horse to the front of his lines, raised his sword, and began the advance. A line of Texans followed him and approached the five-foot Mexican barricade. Within twenty feet of the barricade, Houston hurled his beaver hat high into the air.

"Now," Houston shouted, "Now!"

With the memory of the Alamo in mind, the Americans fought furiously. Although Houston was shot in the leg, he continued to press on.

The terrified Mexicans began to retreat, and in time Santa Anna surrendered. Soon afterwards, Texas became a free territory.

Houston was elected President of the new Republic of Texas. He worked diligently to have Texas admitted to the Union; and later, Sam Houston was elected first United States Senator from Texas.

As the fearful possibility of war among the states grew, Houston spoke strongly against a break in the Union. He ran for Governor of the State of Texas on a platform which vowed to preserve the Union. He won that election. But, in 1861, the Texas Confederates voted to secede from the Union.

Heartbroken, Houston would not act in line with this decision. He knew that by failing to side with the majority, he was ending his political career.

For the rest of his life, Sam Houston continued to fight against civil war and secession. His sincerity and courage made people listen.

When he knew he was dying, he made his will, and left to his son his San Jacinto sword, to be used only, he wrote "in defense of the Constitution and the laws and liberties of his country . . ."

DAVID GLASGOW FARRAGUT
First Rear Admiral

The naval captain paced back and forth over the carpeted floor in his home. From time to time, he muttered something under his breath. His wife, who had been watching him anxiously, put down the tablecloth she was embroidering. "David," she pleaded, "tell me what's troubling you so?"

He shook his head. What was he to tell her—that partly because of her his loyalty to the Union was now in doubt?

"I'm restless," he said. "I've been here at Norfolk since the Civil War broke out, just waiting for orders."

He tried to smile. "I'm not accustomed to idleness. I was a midshipman in the United States Navy before I was 10. You know I began my training at 9 under my father's friend, Captain Porter."

"I know that," his wife answered, "and I'm sure the United States Navy knows it, too. They must remember all your years of service." She stopped for a moment and the color rushed to her face. "David Farragut, I'm going to come right out and say it. I've heard rumors that your orders aren't coming through because I'm from Virginia. They feel that maybe you sympathize with the South because so many of our ties are there."

Farragut's face showed his relief. Now the problem was out in the open. "I'm afraid you're right," he said. Nobody has dared to say anything to my face, but I've heard the same rumors. It seems that the Secretary of the Navy has some doubts about my loyalty to the North.

His wife was indignant. "Your service to your country stands on record."

Of course, she was right. But nobody could know that David Farragut's dreams had fallen to dust. As a young boy, even before he went to sea, he once said to his father, "When I grow up, I'm going to be an admiral."

His father had chuckled. "That's not too likely, Davy, my boy. But if you work hard, who knows?"

He *had* worked hard, very hard. In the War of 1812, Midshipman Farragut sailed on the *Essex* to the Pacific. Later, men spoke of his persistent courage in the terrible battle with two British frigates during which the *Essex* was finally captured.

Years of active duty followed. He fought pirates in the West Indies; he commanded the *Saratoga* in the Mexican War. In 1855, as Captain Farragut, he commanded the new steam sloop *Brooklyn* in the Gulf of Mexico.

Despite his Tennessee birth and other southern bonds, David Farragut believed in the Union. To prove his loyalty, he had uprooted his family and moved north to New York State. Impressed, the U. S. Navy finally gave him his first assignment.

Soon afterwards, Farragut volunteered to take command of a fleet with orders to capture New Orleans, and thus open the mouth of the Mississippi River.

His fleet broke through the enemy's naval defenses and ran past the two forts defending New Orleans. After sinking the enemy ships, he seized the city. A special Act of Congress made David G. Farragut the first Rear Admiral in the United States Fleet.

For the next 16 months, danger was his constant companion. Daily, in the thick of battle, he exhibited bravery.

One day on deck, as Farragut passed a group of his men, the words, "Old Salamander" caught his ear. He turned back and confronted them. "Who's *Old Salamander?*" he asked gruffly.

No one answered.

"Speak up!" the Rear Admiral commanded.

"Damn the torpedoes! Full speed ahead!"

In a low voice, one of the men said, "You, Sir. Excuse me, Sir, it was meant in fun."

Hiding a smile, Farragut said, "May I ask why I've been honored with that particular nickname?"

The same man spoke again. "Well, you see, Sir, a salamander's supposed to be a mythical being who can live in fire." The man swallowed hard. "It's a compliment, Sir."

The men were relieved to see the broad smile on their commanding officer's face.

"Old Salamander," he repeated to himself, "well, well! So that's what they call me."

By December, Farragut held the entire Gulf Coast, except for Mobile—the Confederate's last stronghold.

Farragut anticipated a desperate battle for that city.

His fears were justified. Fort Morgan and Fort Gaines guarded the entrance to Mobile Bay. Rows of torpedoes and mines filled the channel; inside the bay floated the powerful ironclad *Tennessee* and three gunboats.

At the crisis of the battle, the Union's warship *Tecumseh* struck a torpedo and went down, carrying with her nearly all her officers and crew. Defeat was dangerously close.

From one of the officers on the sloop *Brooklyn* rang a warning cry: "Torpedoes ahead!"

With the intuition and skill born of a lifetime at sea, Farragut shouted his now famous order, *"Damn the torpedoes! Full speed ahead!"*

On deck of the *Hartford,* Farragut took the lead through those perilous waters. Although the ship's bottom scraped the torpedoes, miraculously none exploded. Farragut's flagship and his fleet had passed safely into the bay. After a stubborn battle, the Confederate ship *Tennessee* surrendered. Within three hours after the firing of the first gun, the enemy flag was hauled down, and the Stars and Stripes was raised.

The man who had loved the sea since boyhood had once more won a victory. The nation, which he had served well, rewarded his bravery by giving him what he had always dreamed of. In 1866, David Glasgow Farragut was made an Admiral!

KIT CARSON
Frontiersman of the West

Kit Carson leaned against the steamer's rail and puffed on his clay pipe. His eyes took in the muddy water of the Missouri River below.

"Up the Missouri," he thought, "then on to the West. And when I get there...what?" Lost in his thoughts, he did not notice that someone was staring at him. He felt a hand on his shoulder.

"Pardon me," the stranger said, "I'm on a government expedition to the Rockies, but my guide didn't show up. I thought maybe you might know him. His name is Captain Andrew Drips."

"I used to know Andy Drips. We set traps together, but that was some time ago. I can't rightly say where he is now. Reckon he might've been rubbed out by

Injuns. Can't say for sure."

A troubled look had come over the man's face. "I hope not," he said, "but it looks like I'm stuck. I can't go on with the expedition unless I have a trained guide. Oh ... I haven't told you my name. I'm Lieutenant John C. Frémont. I wonder ..." he hesitated, "can you help me?"

"Why is the government sending you to the mountains?" Kit asked bluntly.

Lt. Frémont explained that he was a member of the United States Topographical Engineers Corps. "I'm to explore and chart the interior of North America," he said. "I'm to find resources, possible wagon routes, and locations for forts." Frémont's voice deepened with feeling. "I have a dream that others share with me ... that one day the shores of the American continent will be joined together by roads. But who knows ..." He sighed. "If wagons can't cross the mountains, travel remains impossible."

As Lt. Frémont talked, a faraway look came into Carson's blue eyes. Memories of his past swept through his mind. He had been only a year old when his father had driven their great Conestoga wagon westwards. From Kentucky, the family had ridden in the wagon with everything they owned. More than once, his mother had told him the story. "At last," she would say, "we came to Howard County, Missouri. We were so weary, all of us. Your pa and some of the other men felt the rich soil, and then they walked into the forest to see if there'd be good hunting. Then, we unloaded the wagons . . . and we stayed on."

Kit remembered running through the woods, wild and free as the animals. Although his father hoped to educate his children, no school had been built. Instead of learning to read and write, Kit was learning to shoot straight and to handle his musket with the skill that would be so valuable later on. Gliding silently along in his moccasins, he learned to stalk game, to read the signs of a turned leaf, a flattened blade of grass, a thin wisp of trailing smoke.

Kit's memories raced on. He was only 9 when his father was killed by a falling tree. He would never forget the tears on his mother's cheeks, nor her words: "You must be a man now, son, like your brothers, and help us get along."

The days of running in the forest were over. Kit was obliged to take his turn doing the chores. He spent hours plowing, standing guard against Indians, shucking corn. At other times, he brought home a kill of wild turkey, deer, or even bear.

At 15, he was apprenticed to a saddle maker in Franklin, Missouri. Wistfully his mother had said, "You can't be a lawyer the way your pa wanted for you, but at least you'll have a trade."

Kit feared he would hate being shut up all day in a dark room full of saddles and tools and pieces of leather. Still, his mother was right—he had to help out.

As he had feared, Kit hated being closed up inside all day. His head ached from the dark; his fingers grew sore from the tools. Kit had not realized that Franklin was the stopping off place for caravans headed west. He stared, fascinated, at the mountain men in dirty buckskins who came into the shop for saddle repairs. Eagerly, he listened to their stories of buffalo hunts, of trapping adventures, and of scrapes with the Indians.

Soon the sound of a passing pack train made Kit's heart pound. If only he could live like the fur trappers! When they came to town, their mules' backs loaded with beaver skins to be traded for silver, Kit watched the trappers longingly. His longing grew and grew, until he could fight it no longer. One day, Kit ran away.

While he was reminiscing in this way, Kit heard someone clear his throat. Abruptly, he was brought back to the present. John Frémont was smiling at him. "I'll ask you again," he said, "do you think you can help me?"

Kit Carson hesitated only an instant. "I was deciding about where I was going next," he said. "I'll be proud to guide you, if it suits your notion."

The two men who shook hands on their bargain were as different from each other as two men can be. Of less than medium height, Kit Carson had broad shoulders and a sturdy body. His chin was firm, and his blue eyes level and honest. In contrast to Kit, John Frémont's tall slim body was full of nervous energy. He moved and spoke rapidly.

"I know you by reputation," said Frémont. "But tell me something about yourself."

"I don't mind," said Kit, and he recounted how he had run away from the saddle maker, and how he had joined Charles Bent's wagon train bound for Santa Fe, New Mexico.

"I did some of everything," Kit recalled. "I cooked for the men, drove horses for a while, helped fight the Injuns. I learned how to manage livestock, how to build a fire with anything at hand, how to throw the lasso, and how to handle a long bull whip."

Frémont listened intently to Carson's stories of buffalo hunts and Indian fights. Kit sounded matter of fact as he described the terrible trips through the scorching desert. "After a while," he said, "I got my big chance to be a fur trapper. That's how I come to know the mountains. Guess I'd still be fur trapping if silk toppers hadn't come into fashion and ruined the market for beaver hats."

"Good," said John Frémont. "I'm sure I've found the man I've been looking for!"

Lt. Frémont explained that the object of the expedition was to survey South Pass. "In addition," he said, "we are to take the altitude of the Rockies, and to collect information about the land beyond the frontier."

Anticipation surged in Kit as he thought of the new adventures in store for him. As soon as the steamer docked, Kit went ashore and sent two Delaware runners to Taos, New Mexico with a message. Fifteen of his mountain men were to meet him at Fort Laramie with equipment.

At Fort Laramie, the men reported that the Indians had joined forces against the white men and that great danger awaited the expedition if it ventured any farther into Indian country. "The Indians are out for scalps," the men muttered in rebellion.

"Nonsense," Frémont exclaimed. "We all knew there would be danger. How many men will go with me?" Not a voice, not a hand was raised.

At last Kit Carson said, "I'll go with you, Frémont, after I've made my will." Since his Indian wife had died of fever some time before, he directed that his wages go to his small daughter in St. Louis. Then he picked up his pack and stood ready. Following his example, a number of other trappers picked up their packs, too.

Frémont, with Kit guiding him, safely made the trip to South Pass. By September, 1842, the country had been surveyed and charted; peaks had been measured and named. The party returned to Fort Laramie.

With this job completed, Kit Carson journeyed back to Taos to see once more the young sister-in-law of his first employer, Charles Bent. He could not forget his

first glimpse of the young Spanish beauty, Josefa Jara-
millo. In 1843, he married her.

After he had fulfilled a difficult assignment carrying
a message to Armijo, the Governor of Mexico, Carson
learned that John Frémont wanted him to guide a second expedition.

He could not eagerly say yes. Now he had a lovely
young wife with whom he wanted to stay and build
a life. It was a difficult decision but, at last, Kit decided
to follow his restless urge for adventure.

The second expedition was officially labelled, ''Ex-
ploring Expedition to Oregon and North California in
the year 1843-44.'' They explored the Salt Lake region. But then, when Frémont wanted to push on to
California, most of the mountain men rebelled and returned to Taos. Kit Carson loyally took to the trail with
Frémont. Their expedition finally extended beyond the
boundaries of Oregon and North California, bringing
California into the possession of the United States.

After this survey was completed, Frémont decided to
satisfy his yearning to explore the region between the
Columbia and the Sierras. Again, Kit Carson went with
him.

Southward to the Sierras, the journey grew more
and more difficult. Deep snow and high precipices ham-
pered progress. Often, when it seemed impossible to
take even one more step, Carson cheered the men by
telling them that ''the prettiest valley in the world's

Kit ... attacked a camp of Indian raiders.

right over that ridge. I know ... I was there." They
struggled on. During the 15 days of the trip, some
of the animals starved to death and the men were forced
to live on the carcasses. Desperately worn and haggard,
the starving band finally made Sutter's Fort.

Frémont returned to St. Louis full of praise for Kit
Carson. Enthusiastically, he described one of Kit's most
daring exploits. "With only one other man, Kit had
attacked a camp of Indian raiders. He not only defeated
them but also recovered some of the stolen horses!"
Overnight, Kit Carson became a public hero.

Although more and more pioneers with their wagons were lining the roads to Texas and Oregon, there
still remained work for Frémont and Carson. The pur-

pose of their next expedition was to open a shorter
travel route between northern California and Oregon.
No sooner did they arrive in California than Frémont
and Carson were told by the Mexican commander to
get out of the territory. Although neither Frémont nor
Carson had known it, the Mexican War had begun.

Backed by Carson, Frémont refused to leave. In a
courageous gesture, they raised the American flag; and
the Mexicans did not dare to shoot down the banner.
The sight of the American flag on California soil stirred
Kit deeply.

Later, during the Mexican War, Carson fought
alongside General Stephen Kearny. The war seemed
hopeless for the Americans. In desperation, General

Kearny said to Carson, "Do you think it's possible to slip through the Mexican lines to get reinforcements from San Diego?"

"Maybe," Kit replied.

"Want to try?" the General asked.

"We don't have a chance if I don't," Kit said matter of factly.

For thirty hours, without food or drink, Carson and two other men trudged over rocky terrain to bring help. His rescue mission had been accomplished.

But the career of Carson was not yet over. From 1853 to 1861, he represented the Ute and Apache tribes in their negotiations with white men. Later, he served the American Army in various ways.

One day, Carson was thrown from a horse and suffered severe injuries. Though he thought the time had come for him to rest, word came that the Utes, infuriated by the white man's mistreatment, threatened to go on the war path. Tired and sick as he was, Kit urged the Ute chieftains to accompany him to Washington to see the President of the United States. That was Kit Carson's last mission.

He died in 1868 at the age of 59. He had worked and struggled for a lifetime to help push the American frontier to the Pacific Coast. Neither expecting nor desiring fame, he had simply followed the one rule he had set for himself. "See what needs to be done and then do it!"

ABRAHAM LINCOLN
The Great Emancipator

As far back as he could remember, the seven-year-old boy who had heard his father rail against slavery. Thomas Lincoln was so incensed with that institution that he decided to uproot his wife and two children from their native land in Kentucky and trek to Indiana where the law didn't permit slavery.

The Lincolns arrived in their new home late in the fall. During that first harsh winter, they lived in an untamed country where bears and others wild animals roamed around their house—a little cabin built of logs and poles. Life was brutally hard.

Two years later, the little boy's mother died. Some time thereafter Thomas Lincoln told his children that he must return to Kentucky on business. Abe and his sister, Sarah, were left alone to take care of themselves.

Then one day Abe's father came back home and presented a nice looking woman to the boy and said, "This is your new mother, Abe."

The lady held out her hand and drew the young lad close to her. "I am pleased to know you, son," she said simply. A warm glow suffused the boy. He knew that things would be better now.

Later in life Abraham Lincoln described his early education in these words: "There were some schools, so called, but no qualification was ever required of a teacher beyond readin' writin' and cipherin'." Though few books were available, Abe managed to read the *Bible, Robinson Crusoe, Pilgrim's Progress,* and Weems' *Life of Washington.*

Abe grew tall and lanky, all the way up to six feet, four inches; he was large-boned and strong. His skin was dark; his hair, coarse and black. He was far from a handsome young man, but his eyes shown with intelligence. When he spoke to people gathered at the general store, everyone present listened intently to his stories and jokes.

In 1830, the Lincoln family moved to New Salem, Illinois. Young Abe joined the Militia, which was fighting the Blackhawk War against insurgent Indians. He was elected Captain.

When he returned to New Salem, he was urged to run for the State Legislature. He lost the election.

"Slavery is a moral, social and political evil!"

Then young Lincoln made several attempts at business. He was unsuccessful again and again.

But after these setbacks, he managed to get an appointment as a Postmaster.

Some time later on, the County Surveyor offered to appoint Abe as a deputy. Abe was hesitant. He knew nothing about surveying, but he applied himself diligently to study. In less than six weeks, he mastered the necessary skills and became a competent surveyor.

In 1834, Lincoln again ran for the State Legislature. This time he was elected. Now he had a forum in which he could express his views about the burning issue of the day: "The institution of slavery is founded both on injustice and bad policy," proclaimed the young lawmaker.

During a second term, Lincoln was encouraged to study law. In 1836, he was duly accredited; and one year later he moved to Springfield, Illinois, to become the junior partner in a law firm.

When Lincoln was 33 years old, he married Mary Todd. Four years later, the young and upcoming lawyer was elected to serve a term in Congress. But he decided not to run for re-election. Lincoln had disapproved of the Mexican War, and his outspokenness had stirred resentment among the people he represented.

By then, Abraham Lincoln was a name that was known. When the new Republican Party was organized in Illinois, Lincoln was chosen to run for the United

States Senate against Stephen A. Douglas, a political figure known all over the country. In his acceptance speech, Lincoln said, "A house divided against itself cannot stand! I believe this government cannot endure permanently half slave and half free. I do not expect the house to fall . . . but I *do* expect that it will cease to be divided. It will become all one thing or all the other."

Lincoln then, in a most dramatic move, challenged Douglas to a series of debates. These verbal encounters, most of which were held in the open air, attracted large crowds and great interest. Cried the liberal orator: "Slavery is a moral, social and political evil!" But Douglas won the election.

The loss of the Senate seat in no way diminished Lincoln's growing stature. When the Republicans met at their national convention, Lincoln was nominated for the highest post the country had to offer. The Southerners were steaming in anger. "If Lincoln becomes President," they threatened, "the South will secede from the Union."

And Lincoln was elected.

On March 4, 1861, he took office. Promptly, the southern states acted on their threat. South Carolina was the first to announce that it no longer belonged within the United States. Within a few months, ten other states followed the same course.

A U. S. federal fort, called Fort Sumter, was located in South Carolina. South Carolina claimed that it had the right to occupy and control everything within its sovereign territory. The state demanded the surrender of Fort Sumter. The United States officers in charge refused. General Beauregard, the southern general, attacked and captured the fort. With this act, the Civil War began.

Now North and South were locked in deadly struggle, with brother fighting against brother. It was to be a long and bitter war with many casualties on both sides.

On January 1, 1863, Abraham Lincoln issued his now famous Emancipation Proclamation which declared that all slaves in the rebellious states were free. This proclamation in itself did not, as a matter of law, wipe out slavery in every part of the United States; the proclamation applied only to the states which had seceded from the Union. But the proclamation paved the way for the 13th·Amendment to the Constitution of the United States, which forever outlawed slavery in every part of the country.

The fateful battle of the war was fought in the town of Gettysburg, Pennsylvania, in 1863. This was the turning point. On November 19th of that year, a military cemetery was dedicated on the spot where, in effect, the Union was saved.

Lincoln arose to make his little speech which he had scribbled down on the back of an envelope. That speech is learned today by school children throughout the

width and breadth of the United States. The address
ended with the memorable words, "that we here highly
resolve that these dead shall not have died in vain; that
this nation, under God, shall have a new birth of freedom; and that government of the people, by the people
and for the people shall not perish from the earth."

In 1864, Lincoln was re-elected to the presidency.
In his second inaugural speech, the Great Emancipator
called for "malice toward none and charity for all." He
implored the people "to bind up the nation's wounds,
to care for him who shall have borne the battle, for his
widow and his orphan, to do all which may achieve a
just and lasting peace . . ."

. . . a bullet shot exploded through the theatre . . .

On April 9, 1865, General Robert E. Lee, Commander of the forces of the South, surrendered to General Ulysses S. Grant, Commander-in-Chief of the Union Army. The Civil War was over.

Five days later, the President went to Ford's Theatre in Washington to see a play. A little after ten o'clock, a bullet shot exploded through the theatre: an actor, John Wilkes Booth, had assassinated the President.

Lincoln never regained consciousness. Surrounded by his grieving family and friends, he died the next morning.

The nation was stricken. The grief it felt was best expressed by Walt Whitman who wrote the following elegy:

> *O Captain! my Captain! our fearful trip is done,*
> *The ship has weather'd every rack, the prize we*
> *   sought is won,*
> *The port is near, the bells I hear, the people all*
> *   exulting,*
> *While follow eyes the steady keel, the vessel*
> *   grim and daring;*
> *   But O heart! heart! heart!*
> *   O the bleeding drops of red,*
> *   Where on the deck my Captain lies,*
> *   Fallen cold and dead.*
>
> *O Captain! my Captain! rise up and hear the*
> *   bells;*

Rise up—for you the flag is flung—for you the
  bugle trills,
For you bouquets and ribbon'd wreaths—for you
  the shores a-crowding,
For you they call, the swaying mass, their eager
  faces turning;
    Here Captain! dear father!
      This arm beneath your head!
        It is some dream that on the deck,
          You've fallen cold and dead.

My Captain does not answer, his lips are pale
  and still,
My father does not feel my arm, he has no pulse
  nor will,
The ship is anchor'd safe and sound, its voyage
  closed and done,
From fearful trip the victor ship comes in with
  object won;
    Exult O shores, and ring O bells!
      But I with mournful tread,
        Walk the deck my Captain lies,
          Fallen cold and dead.

Today, thousands of people visit Oak Ridge Cemetery in Springfield, Illinois, to pay homage to one of the greatest of all Americans. Today, even more thousands in number visit the Lincoln Memorial in Washington, D.C., to pay their respects to the man who laid the foundations for racial equality.

ROBERT E. LEE
Leader in Reconciliation

The General, in the gray full dress uniform of the Confederate Army, sat straight and tall on his gray thoroughbred. His leather boots shone, and the scabbard holding his sword gleamed. By his grim face and the pain in his eyes one could tell that this was a hard hour.

In the McLean House at Appomattox, Virginia on April 9, 1865 General Robert E. Lee, commander of the Confederate Army, surrendered formally to General Ulysses S. Grant, commander of the Union Army.

The defeated General rode back to his camp, where he was surrounded by groups of his soldiers, gaunt men in rags of uniforms. These strong men, who had fought a hard war and endured untold misery without complaint, now wept openly, unashamed.

The Civil War was over. The years of strife had come to an end. What lay in store for him and his torn land, Robert E. Lee could not tell. But he vowed to dedicate himself to the ways of peace and to the healing of the wounds of the nation.

From his early childhood in Stratford, Virginia, he could recall his awe of relatives who had fought for their country's independence in the Revolutionary War. His own father, Henry Lee, known as Lighthorse Harry, had been a famous Revolutionary War leader and had been personally acquainted with George Washington.

Lee's mother had come from a prominent family; Robert was brought up with a sense of tradition that would remain with him al his life. The qualities of honor, good citizenship, and loyalty to the state—he accepted without question.

Despite the patrician background, the Lee family had more troubles. But the lack of money, the need to care for his sick mother, and the necessity of taking over a man's responsibilities in the abesnce of his father, only helped to make Robert E. Lee an extraordinary person. And it was his mother who instilled in him the qualities of humility, faith, and kindness which contributed to his greatness.

Attending the Alexandria Academy where tuition was free, Robert studied Greek, Latin, and Mathematics, doing especially well in Algebra and Geometry.

When he was graduated, Robert knew where he

wanted to go. He confided in his mother. "I would like to try for West Point," he said.

He could tell that she approved his choice, but a sober expression came over her worn face. "So many worthy young men are turned away each year; it will not be to your discredit if you are one of them." Robert hoped desperately that he would be one of the fortunate ones. For one thing, West Point was free. For another, lack of money would make it difficult for him to acquire further schooling elsewhere. Robert E. Lee was accepted at West Point and graduated in 1829 with high honors. Several years later, he married Mary Ann Randolph Custis, the great granddaughter of George Washington's wife, Martha.

During the next few years, Lee was involved with engineering jobs for the United States Army. He took charge of the engineering plans for the St. Louis harbor, and for the upper Mississippi and Missouri Rivers.

When the War with Mexico broke out, Lee was called to San Antonio, Texas, as Assistant Engineer to the Army. There he supervised the building of bridges. Because of his unusual engineering skill, American troops were able to cross dangerous mountain passes on their way to Mexico City. He was promoted three times; before the end of the war, he had reached the rank of Colonel.

General Winfield Scott made public the statement that his own "success in Mexico was largely due to the

skill, valor and undaunted courage of Robert E. Lee . . .
the greatest military genius in America."

After the Mexican War, Lee became the Superin-
tendent of West Point. During his three years at the
U.S. Military Academy, he impressed the students with
his fairness and understanding.

For some time, the slavery issue in the United States
had grown in importance. Robert E. Lee had been out-
spoken in his condemnation of that shameful institution. "It is evil," he said, "and its evils are perhaps worse
for the whites who own slaves than for the Negroes
who are forced into slavery." Some years before the war,
he had freed the small number of slaves in his household.

Gradually it became clear that a peaceful solution of
the slavery problem would not be easy. The threat of
war between the states caused Lee great anguish. If war
came, what was he to do? Yes, he was loyal to the
Union; but his beloved state, Virginia, also commanded
his fidelity. He pondered the problem in an agony of
indecision.

As one state after another seceded, Lee's torment increased. After painful deliberation he wrote a letter to
a relative: "I wish to live under no other government,
and there is no sacrifice I am not ready to make for the
preservation of the Union, save that of honor. If a dis-
ruption takes place, I shall go back to my native state
and serve in her defense."

Shortly afterwards, his old commander, General
Scott, offered Lee the field command of the United
States Army. It was difficult to refuse. Lee admired General Scott and Scott was his friend. But the thought of
fighting his own people sickened him; he knew that
was something he could never do.

Things then moved swiftly. Jefferson Davis, the
newly elected President of the Confederacy, was well
aware of Lee's military genius. Davis appointed Lee as
his military advisor with the rank of General.

Although Lee did not fight in the first battle of Ma-
nassas, he had formulated its strategy and was, there-
fore, partly responsible for the resulting Confederate
victory.

The defeated General rode back to his camp, where he was surrounded by groups of his soldiers . . .

In June 1862, Lee took command of the Confederate Armies in the Virginia peninsula. In a series of battles near Richmond, he drove General George B. McClellan's Union troops from the Confederate capital.

Along with General "Stonewall" Jackson, Lee won an important victory at the Battle of Bull Run. But each victory took its toll in men and blood. The victory at Chancellorsville turned out to be a tragedy—General Jackson was fatally wounded; and worst of all, as the war went on the Confederate reserves were seriously diminished. Lee was certain that the defensive battles his forces were fighting could not win the war.

Lee determined to take the offensive. He led his troops into Pennsylvania, where the critical Battle of Gettysburg was fought. The struggle lasted for three days. The Confederates lost, and retreated across the Potomac River. Although Lee's officers had made serious tactical mistakes, Lee himself insisted on taking all the blame for the failure.

In the Spring of 1864, after the cruelest winter of the war, the Confederates met the Union Army, then under the command of General Ulysses S. Grant. Fierce battles took place in May and early June. Losses on both sides were very, very heavy; but the North with its greater population, had more men to lose than the South. Ultimaely, Lee could not bear to sacrifice his men in a cause that seemed hopeless. Withdrawing his armies from Petersburg and Richmond, Lee accepted Grant's surrender terms.

As a private citizen, his first act was to take an oath of allegiance to the United States Government. Then, in a ringing speech to his Southern countrymen, he advocated, "Abandon your animosities and make your sons Americans!" Here was a man who recognized his unique responsibility to the nation, and particularly to the South.

After the Civil War ended, Robert E. Lee did everything in his power to rebuild the South. He encouraged his Southern neighbors to abandon their hatred of the Northerner and to turn to brotherhood.

In 1865, Robert E. Lee accepted the Presidency of Washington College at Lexington, Virginia. He did this because he "wanted to educate Southern youth in a spirit of loyalty to the new conditions."

As President, he took over the ruins of a school. The library had been destroyed; lab equipment had been broken; buildings had been looted and left in disrepair. Undaunted, Robert E. Lee took care of his own correspondence, oversaw the remodeling of buildings and the beautifying of the school grounds, and worked to raise money to keep the school going.

The most important work he did, however, was with the student body. He taught young people the meaning of honor and courage. Urging them to support the federal government he said, "You cannot be a man until you learn to obey."

Although he was not an old man, the years of war had undermined Lee's strength. Early in 1870, Lee's health began to fail. He died on October 12, 1870.

After his death, Washington College paid him tribute by adding his name to the institution. Now Washington and Lee University is a lasting memorial to its former President.

Robert E. Lee's place in history does not primarily rest on his reputation as a great general. He will be remembered because, out of defeat, this man rose to greater heroism as a man who swallowed defeat and worked toward peace.

BOOKER T. WASHINGTON
Pioneering Negro Educator

Before Abraham Lincoln freed the Negro slaves, the colored children of America did not go to school. They worked from morning till night at carrying wood, feeding pigs, picking cotton, and similar labor. They received no eduation and grew up without knowing how to read or write.

But going to school was exactly what one little colored boy wanted more than anything else in the world, ever since he first carried his white mistress' schoolbooks, and first looked inside the schoolhouse door. "It must be paradise," the little boy thought. "And just as hard to get into!"

But he resolved to win a chance to study as the white children were doing. This little boy was Booker T.

Washington. The burning ambition to study never left him—not even when his people were freed, and he had to work beside grown men in a coal mine.

Booker was but ten years old. He hated the dirty, dangerous work, down in the depths of the earth, with big rats scuttling through the black caverns. But one day, a bright ray of hope shined down into that dark mine. That day, Booker overheard some mine workers talking. He trembled with excitement at what they were saying. He got down on his hands and knees and crawled as close as he dared to the voices. There was a new school, they said; it was called the *Hampton Institute.* There, colored boys and girls could earn their keep, while they studied. The school did not teach Latin or Greek; it trained the students in valuable trades so that they could earn a decent living.

Six years later, in 1874, the schoolmistress of that school stared in amazement at a dirty, bedraggled boy who appeared before her. Booker, now sixteen years old, had travelled *five hundred miles* in order that he might have an education. To start his journey, he had saved some money working as a servant. When the money gave out, he trudged doggedly on foot, sleeping wherever he could at night, begging rides in carts, wagons, or whatever came along. In Richmond, Virginia, he loaded pig-iron during the day and slept nights without shelter. Now here he stood, with nothing but a little satchel of clothes, fifty cents in his

Now here he stood, with nothing but a little satchel of clothes . . . and a determination to succeed.

pocket, a heart bursting with joy, and a determination to succeed.

The boy's dishevelled appearance made a poor impression on Miss Mackie, the schoolteacher, but he had come so far that she decided to give him a chance. She asked him to clean a schoolroom. When she saw how thoroughly he removed every speck of dust from the room, she accepted him into the school as a student.

Booker was given the job of janitor. He rose every morning at four to light the school's fires and study his lessons. He cleaned the schoolrooms at night. Step by step, the young man advanced his knowledge. By diligent study and by dint of great desire, his mind grew in power. He became interested not alone in educating himself, but fired by the ambition of educating all of his Negro brothers who had been reared in ignorance.

When only twenty-six, Booker T. Washington opened a school in a little shanty which he called Tuskeegee Institute. He beckoned to his colored brethren to come and drink of the fountain of learning. Though the school started with but a few students, it grew in time to be a world-famous institution.

Here is a truly incredible story—the story of a slave boy who became the founder of a renowned college. It is the story of a boy who fought against the greatest odds and by sheer will power worked his way up to become one of the respected leaders of his day. He will always be remembered as an inspiration of what can be done by steadfastness of heart and steadfastness of purpose.

ROBERT E. PEARY

Discoverer of the North Pole

"Have you checked the harnesses?" cried a voice through the chill Arctic air.

"Yes, they're all in order, sir," came back the reply.

"Are the sleds all loaded?"

"Not completely, sir. We'll need another ten minutes."

"Take all the time you need, but do a good job."

The man who was issuing the orders was about six feet tall, dressed in a fur suit, wearing heavy Arctic boots, thick leather gloves, and a fur hood. He was Commander Robert E. Peary of the United States Navy. As he stood gazing at the bustling activity which seethed around him, at the fur-clothed men running back and forth, loading, unloading, shouting to each other, fastening ropes and harnesses, tying up dogs, tripping over the yelping animals as they ran underfoot —gazing at the last-minute preparations for the long journey that lay ahead—Peary drew in his breath sharply.

His glance wandered to the strange white wilderness that lay around him, the glittering, endless plain of snow and ice, the bare white sky. Excitement shone in his eyes. "This is it," he said to himself. "This is my last chance. It's now or never! This time I *must* find it."

Find *it!* Find *what?* It was the very top of the world that Peary wanted to reach, the great mystery of the north that he wanted to solve! To be the first man to reach the North Pole was a dream that had possessed courageous men before him and lured them to their doom. Peary himself had tried many times before and failed. Yet, despite the severe hardships he had endured, despite the discouragement that came with each new failure, despite the terrors of the ice north that had thrust him back before he had reached his goal, he had still found the courage to say, "One day I *will* succeed!"

Twenty-two years earlier, Peary had made his first expedition to the Arctic. As a young naval officer he had chanced to pick up a little pamphlet on Arctic exploration in a second-hand bookstore. That night, as he lay in bed reading, he was captured by a dream! He knew that he must go to the Arctic—to see it, to explore it, to travel where no man had ever been before! That same year, 1886, he set out on his first expedition into the interior of Greenland. He had a young Dane and eight Eskimos as companions.

For weeks he travelled through barren wastes of snow and ice, getting his first taste of the kind of life he would lead for many years to come. He had chosen a good training ground, for a large portion of the huge island of Greenland lay well within the Arctic Circle. As a matter of fact, no one even knew how far north Greenland extended, for in 1886 no one had yet reached its northern boundaries.

To find these boundaries became the aim of Peary's second expedition which set forth in 1891. With him, this time, went his wife and six men. They started off with high hopes. But a month after they left New York, as their ship was ramming its way through some thick ice, the vessel's iron tiller struck Peary's leg and broke it in two places.

Peary refused to call off the expedition. Two weeks afterward, when the party landed on Greenland, Peary had to be carried ashore on a stretcher. Though he could not walk, Peary, from his bed, directed the building of a house and the setting up of the entire camp. Six months later, the northern boundaries of Greenland were discovered!

But Peary had decided to settle for nothing less than the North Pole itself. In 1893, he set out on a new expedition; and once again in 1896; and again in 1897.

In 1898, he had a special ship built, a ship geared for Arctic exploration. Seven hundred miles away from the Pole the ship became ice-bound. The party disembarked and set up camp. Peary's feet became so severely frostbitten that eight toes had to be cut off, but he refused to call off the expedition. In a few weeks, he was walking again. For three-and-a-half years more he stayed in the Arctic, returning to the United States in 1902. The goal had been approached but not as yet conquered.

Three years later, in 1905, Commander Peary started out again. The party spent the winter in camp, as usual, and set off for the Pole in the spring. For the first two weeks, they made fine progress. But one day they found their path completely blocked. They had encountered a region of *leads*. Leads are wide lanes of water in the ice. The party could travel across ice and snow, but it was impossible for the men, sledges, and dogs to cross the water. They could do nothing but wait until the leads closed up. Waiting meant using up valuable supplies while they stayed in one place.

When they were able to proceed once more, their dogs were exhausted and their food supply was extremely low. Again the Arctic had defeated them. There was nothing to do but turn around and make their way back to camp, discouraged and worn ragged by a most dreadful trip.

But Peary was a man who would not recognize defeat. For twenty years, he had devoted all his time, all his money, all his energy, all his hopes and skill to conquering the Arctic. He was getting older. He was fifty. Soon he would have to give up. But one more try he was bound to have!

As soon as he got back to the United States, he started organizing another expedition. But it was not until he was fifty-two years old that everything was in order. So now in the spring of 1909, as his party made ready to leave the winter camp, Peary stood watching his men load the sledges and harness the dogs for a last dash to the Pole. He knew it was his last chance. This time he *had* to reach his goal.

With all the knowledge gained through years of exploration, Peary and his companions forged a path through the Arctic wasteland. Everything went well: the weather was good, the travelling not too difficult. Prospects were bright, when suddenly they hit their old enemy—the leads! For fourteen days they waited impatiently for the leads to close up. Then they set off once more. They had reached a point further north than any man had ever been before. To conserve supplies, Peary sent back everyone except five men: four Eskimos and his Negro aide, Mathew Henson, who had been by his side on every Arctic expedition he had ever made, except the first one to Greenland. The six men trudged on. The weather remained favorable. On the morning of April 6th, they found themselves only

*On top of a mound of ice and snow . . . Peary planted
the American flag.*

three miles from the Pole. At last, Peary knew he was going to succeed. They rested and then went on. In a few hours, they were there. On top of a mound of ice and snow which he built himself, Peary planted the American flag. The moment of victory had finally come!

It had taken twenty-two years and eight expeditions, but he had made it! The broken leg, the frozen feet, the bitter cold, the agonies of pain, the disappointments, the heartaches, had all been worth it. *He had made it!* North, east, and west had all disappeared. There was only one direction now: *south*. For Peary was at the North Pole and *Old Glory* was flying on top of the world.

SERGEANT YORK
America's One-man Army

"Sergeant Early!"

"Yes, Captain?"

"We're in a tough spot! There are Germans on three sides of us. If we don't get out of here now, every last one of us will be wiped out. Take a few men with you and see if you can find a way of escape. There isn't a minute to lose!"

The men of the 328th Regiment, fighting in a decisive battle in northern France, had been cut off from the rest of the American army. They were trapped in a small valley in the forest. German machine guns blazed at them from three directions. The men hid as best they could among the trees. Casualties mounted; it became obvious that they could not hold out long.

Following the Captain's orders, Sergeant Early selected a handful of men to find an escape route for the trapped regiment. Among these men was a young red-headed corporal from Tennessee named Alvin York.

The soldiers picked their way noiselessly through the woods. They slipped behind the German gun emplacements. Sergeant Early stopped suddenly. "Do you see what I see?" he whispered. "Take a look at the far bank of the stream!"

A group of German soldiers were standing before a little hut talking to some officers.

"We must attack instantly," muttered Early. "If they see us first, we're lost! Spread out! When I give the signal, charge and shoot!"

Silently, the Americans took their positions. Then, at their leader's signal, they dashed toward the stream. The astounded Germans tried to return fire, but they had been caught completely by surprise. In a few moments fifteen Americans had captured more than thirty Germans!

Quickly, the Americans disarmed their prisoners and lined them up. Immediately from many directions came a withering hail of bullets. The Americans dropped on their stomachs to escape the terrible onslaught. But the attack had been violent and unexpected. Six men were killed and three wounded.

Sergeant Early was severely hurt. His pain was so terrible that, as he lay in agony, he had to gasp out his orders: "Corporal York! Take command!"

Sergeant Early could not have picked a better man. Alvin York had been brought up in the mountains of Tennessee, where every mountaineer learns, as a boy, to shoot a rifle. York had been the best shot in his home county and he knew the forest well. His ears could tell the difference between a man's lightest footstep and a rabbit's leap. Glancing about, he saw the desperation of his patrol's position. The thirty German prisoners grinned secretly. They were certain they would be rescued. And York knew that unless they were carefully guarded, they would turn on the Americans and kill them.

"Guard the prisoners!" York shouted. "I'll handle all oncomers myself. Leave the shooting to me!"

York's comrades hardly believed their ears. Did the Corporal plan to attack the mass of Germans single-handed?

But they did not know Alvin York. The young, red-headed six-footer from the Tennessee mountains intended to do exactly that.

With quiet determination, he flattened himself against a nearby tree. He knew that if he made the slightest movement, he would be instantly mowed down by machine guns. Grimly, he aimed his rifle. Whenever he spied a moving shape, he fired.

The hand of an ordinary man might have faltered. But not that of Alvin York. His keen eyes spotted the

Germans through the trees. He aimed and fired, barely pausing between shots. Twenty-five times he fired his gun and every shot, except one, brought down a German.

Terror struck the German soldiers. Who was this man who could hit twenty-four men out of twenty-five? In a burst of fury, eight Germans suddenly appeared from a hilltop dugout. Led by an officer, they rushed down the hill, determined to wipe out this American.

Alvin York took aim. He fired his first shot when the Germans were still twenty yards away. Down went the first German. On came the other seven. Again he aimed. And again. Eight times he fired, and eight Germans lay dead.

Then a German major came out from behind the German lines. "Cease fire!" he shouted. "Just stop shooting and we will surrender!"

From behind trees and rocks and bushes the Germans poured, hands above their heads. "Kamerad!" they shouted. "Kamerad! We surrender!"

The half-dozen Americans stared unbelievingly. When they had disarmed the Germans, they had ninety-two prisoners!

But even as the Americans rejoiced over their astounding victory, York warned: "We're in enemy territory. The woods are full of Germans. We were cut to pieces before. We must get out of here with our prisoners."

He made the German prisoners march directly ahead of him, his gun pointed at their backs. Before they had gone very far, they stumbled on a cluster of German machine gunners. When the Germans saw the ninety-two prisoners, they supposed that an entire American regiment must be behind them. They did not dare aim at the Americans for fear they might hit their own men. So they, too, surrendered and joined the procession.

"Cease fire! . . . Just stop shooting and we will surrender!"

When they came to the next German machine gun nest, the same thing happened. The Germans, believing themselves greatly outnumbered, merely raised their hands in surrender.

By the time York reached the American lines he had one hundred and thirty German prisoners. And thirty-five machine guns had been put out of action.

An American major gasped when he saw the prisoners. "This is impossible!" he cried. "I must be dreaming. Do you mean to tell me that you six men captured these Germans?"

"No," replied Sergeant Early. "Just *one* man captured them: Corporal York, sir. Never have I seen such courage and skill. Why, he was a regular one-man army!"

When York's superior officers heard of his deed, he was promoted to the rank of sergeant. He was decorated with the highest medal awarded a military man, the Congressional Medal of Honor.

And when Sergeant York returned to the United States, he received the most rousing welcome ever given to an American soldier. Throughout America, the story was told and retold, thrilling the hearts of Americans everywhere.

FRANKLIN DELANO ROOSEVELT
The Man Who Conquered Paralysis

At last, the days and nights of agonized waiting had come to an end. The patient's head no longer burned with fever; his terrible headache was gone. But for Franklin Delano Roosevelt another kind of agony had barely begun.

"I can't move my legs," he said desperately to his wife Eleanor who sat near his bed.

The compassion on her face told him that she knew.

"Will I walk again . . . ever?" he asked, trusting that she would tell him the truth.

"Yes," she said, "but it will take time."

How much time, not even the doctors could foretell. Many victims of infantile paralysis remained crippled for life. Franklin Roosevelt did not guess that never again would he walk normally, without a cane or brace.

The only son of James and Sara Delano Roosevelt, Franklin had been brought up in an atmosphere of wealth and ease. The family name, which also belonged to his fifth cousin, Theodore Roosevelt, was an old aristocratic name. Before his illness, Roosevelt's interest in politics had won him the position of Assistant Secretary of the Navy in 1914. Later, in 1920, he won the Democratic nomination for Vice President. Franklin Roosevelt was a man blessed by good fortune, both in his personal and political life. Then the cruel and crushing illness—infantile paralysis—struck away his health and, with his health, his political hopes.

During the painful months of convalescence, Franklin Roosevelt said many times with a regret he tried to conceal, "Politics are over for me. A man who can't walk doesn't belong in public life."

His longing to walk brought him to Warm Springs, Georgia where victims of paralyzing diseases were treated. There, to his great joy, he found that swimming in the warm pool helped his useless muscles. Slowly, slowly some strength began to come back to his legs.

While Roosevelt was trying to regain his health, he could not help but look around him. What he saw aroused his warm sympathy. Many crippled youngsters from poor families were not getting the same kind of treatment and care he was. With some of his old vigor,

Roosevelt decided to do something for these stricken children. The "something" led to the establishment of the Warm Springs Foundation to provide care and treatment for the crippled, especially for those who could not pay.

In spite of his own withdrawal from politics, Franklin Roosevelt had kept in touch with the political scene. He knew how deeply his old friend Al Smith hoped to gain the presidential nomination on the Democratic ticket. He knew, too, that Smith would need all the help his friends could give him.

It was Franklin Delano Roosevelt who nominated Al Smith at the Democratic National Convention in a rousing powerful speech. In the speech, Roosevelt described Al Smith, a hard-hitting democrat with a sense of humor, as "The Happy Warrior." It was the first of many apt phrases Roosevelt was to utter, phrases that pleased people and stuck in their memories. The eloquence and beauty of Roosevelt's oratory enormously impressed the members of the convention. Al Smith won the nomination.

Several days later, Al Smith said to Roosevelt, "We want you to run for governor of New York." Roosevelt could hardly believe his ears. "Me!" he exclaimed. "You must be joking." He pointed to his cane. "I'm still crippled . . ." His voice lowered and with visible pain he added, "I know now that to some degree I always shall be." But Al Smith and the Democratic party were not joking!

When Roosevelt expressed his fears to his wife about running for governor of New York, she said with quiet wisdom, "Your brain isn't crippled. Neither is your heart. Listen to them!"

Suddenly, overriding his misgivings, a secret exultation took possession of him. Governor of New York! —the possibility excited his imagination. The Roosevelt family had made New York its home for generations. Why there were even Roosevelts in New Amsterdam, as New York was called in colonial days. His wife was watching him anxiously. He turned to her and smiled. "Yes," he said, "I'll tell Al Smith that I agree to run."

Much to Franklin Roosevelt's surprise, although Al Smith lost the presidential election, Roosevelt won the governorship of New York, his first important political office. It was up to him to prove the voters' wisdom in electing him. Although he was to use a cane, braces, or a wheelchair for the rest of his life, Roosevelt felt that his illness now belonged to the past. People had always interested him. As their governor, he could show the people that they had elected a liberal who would fight for them.

Working long hours, Roosevelt came to be known as the outstanding liberal of the Democratic Party. When elections came again, New Yorkers re-elected Governor Roosevelt by a tremendous majority.

By 1932, the United States was in the midst of the worst economic depression in the country's history. Hundreds of thousands were out of work. Daily, the people grew more frightened. New economic disasters loomed before them. They needed a leader to give them hope—and jobs.

Roosevelt was aware that, as governor, his farm relief program and liberal policies had aroused the interest of the nation. It did not come as a complete surprise when the leaders of the Democratic Party asked him to run for President.

Once more, the old doubts plagued Roosevelt. The presidency of the United States was the most important job in the world. Could he step in and help his country recover from its desperate economic situation?

As always, the faith of his family and good friends helped him. At last, he saw clearly where his future responsibilities lay. "I'll do it," Roosevelt told his wife and children, "and may God help me!" Franklin D. Roosevelt swept into office, defeating Herbert Hoover by a popular majority of nearly seven million votes.

Three weeks earlier, a bank panic had begun. Many banks closed their doors. Overnight people had lost their life savings.

The time had come for Franklin Roosevelt to deliver his campaign pledge. It was a brave pledge. He promised a desperate nation not only to lift it out of its present depression but also to safeguard the nation

"All we have to fear is fear itself!"

from any future depression.

The man who had faced first death and then complete paralysis, stood staunchly on his braces before a terrified people and made his inaugural address of 1933. He knew from his own experience how paralyzing fear can be. With vivid personal knowledge Roosevelt said, "All we have to fear is fear itself!" His sincerity gave the nation confidence.

In his first years as President, Roosevelt proposed many measures to the Congress. The new measures became known as *The New Deal.* The people liked and approved of his social reforms. One of his most important pieces of legislation was the Social Security Act.

Frequently, he used the radio to speak directly to his countrymen. These eagerly awaited talks became known as FDR's "Fireside Chats."

In 1936, the people re-elected Roosevelt for a second term as President of the United States.

Although matters in America were greatly improving, a new cloud hung over the world. Europe was on the threshold of war. Roosevelt felt that the United States could not shut its eyes to the world's tragedy. When World War II broke out in 1939, he was determined to provide all aid, short of war, to the nations fighting the German and Italian dictatorships. Appalled by Italy's invasion of France on June 10, 1940, Roosevelt condemned the aggressive act in these dramatic words: "The hand that held the dagger has struck it into the back of its neighbor!"

The dangerous plight of his country and the world made him decide to run for a third term. And he won an overwhelming election victory.

On December 7, 1941, the Japanese Air Force sprang a surprise attack on the American Pacific Fleet in Pearl Harbor, Hawaii. President Roosevelt told a shocked and frightened nation that he had no choice but to declare war on Japan and her Axis partners, Germany and Italy. His voice choked with emotion as he said, "This day of infamy will live in our nation's history."

Now the United States was involved in the most terrible war in history. Few families were spared the anguish of parting from their loved ones. For months, things went badly with the Allies—England, France, Russia, and the United States. Roosevelt had many conferences with England's Winston Churchill and Russia's Josef Stalin. Together, the three leaders founded the United Nations, an organization of nations whose purpose was to prevent future wars and to promote peace.

The years of illness and grave responsibility had left their mark on Franklin Roosevelt. His face was lined and tired. Often in a wheelchair now, he moved with pain he was barely able to conceal. In common with other parents, he faced the possible loss of his four sons, all of whom had enlisted in active service.

Though they dreaded the effects on Roosevelt of a fourth term in the White House, his friends dared not advise him. Countless times, Roosevelt asked himself the same question, "What shall I do?" His answer: "The country is still at war. I can't rest until we have achieved victory!"

But he did not live to see that victory. On April 12, 1945, less than four months after he took office for his fourth term as President of the United States, Franklin Delano Roosevelt died of a cerebral hemorrhage. People all over the world wept as if they had suffered a personal loss. An entire generation of Americans had grown up during Roosevelt's presidency. His fascinating life and his achievements in the face of suffering had inspired millions. Years later, people relived his early life in a play called *Sunrise at Campobella,* depicting how he had overcome the burdens of polio. The play became a Broadway hit.

Franklin Delano Roosevelt was laid to rest at the Roosevelt family home in Hyde Park, New York, which has since become a national shrine, visited each year by thousands.

ERNIE PYLE
Front Line Reporter

When World War II began in Europe, a newspaper man named Ernie Pyle wrote in his daily column, "A small voice came in the night and said *Go.*" Ernie Pyle obeyed his inner voice and went off to war.

The war correspondent's job is to travel to the front and report to the people at home what is happening to the fighting men. Ernie Pyle became the best loved columnist of World War II.

He wrote about the ordinary soldier, nicknamed the GI. He told how the GI lived, what he wore, what he ate. He told about the GI's problems, his fears, and his dreams. Dressed in coveralls and a wool cap like any GI, Ernie Pyle spent night after night shivering with cold in his bedroll. He learned to do what the GI's did.

In his column he wrote, "It wasn't long before I could put up my tent all by myself in the dark with a strong wind howling and both hands tied behind my back."

Who was this Ernie Pyle of whom President Harry Truman said, "More than any other man, he became the spokesman of the American in arms"? Who was this man who won a Pulitzer Prize in 1943 for war reportage? Most important, who was this man who chose to spend a significant part of his life telling the story of the American foot soldier in World War II?

Ernie Pyle was born in Dana, Indiana. After studying journalism at Indiana University, he took a job as a small town reporter on the La Porte, Indiana *Herald Argus*. From there, he went to the copy desk of the District of Columbia *Washington News*. In 1932, he was appointed managing editor of that metropolitan daily.

The managing editorship was a responsible job, and Ernie was a successful editor. But a gnawing restlessness nagged at him. He was familiar with this restlessness. In 1935, with his wife, Jerry, Ernie took a long trip to the southwest. There, he found himself intrigued by the unfamiliar countryside and by the different kinds of people he met. He wrote to the editor-in-chief of the *News* asking for assignments as a roving reporter.

After reading his first columns, the Scripps Howard editor-in-chief offered the opinion that "they had a sort of Mark Twain quality, and they knocked my eyes right out!"

*—a German bomber made a direct hit on
Press Headquarters.*

Pyle's travel columns began to appear in Scripps
Howard papers everywhere in America. For the next
five years, Ernie wandered all over the western hem-
isphere. He wrote with a quiet humor and sympathy,
with an intimacy that made his readers think of him as
a friend.

Then came World War II. First, Ernie spent time
in England; later he traveled with the troops to North
Africa. In 1943, he turned eastward to Tunisia. He was
bombed and shelled. Once, he was the target of a German machine gunner who narrowly missed him.

From North Africa, Ernie went to Italy. There on
the Anzio beachhead came his closest brush with death

—a German bomber made a direct hit on Press Headquarters. Miraculously, Ernie escaped. He then returned
to England for D Day.

During his constant encounters with danger, Ernie
began to feel a terrible premonition of death. To a
friend he wrote, "Instead of becoming used to danger,
I become less used to it as the years go by. I've begun to
feel I have about used up my chances."

It was important that he go home to America. From
France he wrote in his farewell column, "My spirit is
wobbly and my mind is confused . . . All of a sudden it
seemed to me that if I heard one more shot or saw one
more dead man, I would go off my nut."

Ernie returned to the United States. Being home was good. But gradually the feeling grew that he must go back. Ernie spoke honestly about his return. "I dread going back," he said, "and I'd give anything if I didn't have to go, but I feel I have no choice. I feel a sense of duty toward the soldiers. I've become their mouthpiece —the only one they have." And so he returned to the warfront—this time to the Pacific—because he felt that was where the heaviest fighting was going on.

On the island of Iwo Jima near Okinawa, just before he was killed, Ernie Pyle wrote his last column about GI Joe. This gentle, modest man, whose quiet dignity had impressed everyone who ever knew him, had brought the story of the common soldier home to America.

THE FOUR CHAPLAINS

Soldiers in the Army of the Lord

The soldiers sat up sharply on their bunks. The cry had just been heard, "German submarine ahead!" In tense silence, they looked at each other, each one concealing as best he could fear that gripped his heart.

Then suddenly, the giant ship heaved and trembled as a torpedo cut a jagged, gaping hole in its side. With a roar, the water rushed into the hold. Then another torpedo struck—and another!

In desperate haste, the men of the U.S.S. Dorchester put on their life-jackets. When the order "Abandon ship!" boomed over the loudspeaker a few moments later, the decks were covered with a panicky swarm of men, struggling desperately into life-jackets, stumbling, shouting, running toward the lifeboats. As an icy wind whistled between the masts and funnels, frightened soldiers jumped overboard into the freezing North Atlantic.

But throughout this terrible confusion, four men calmly went among the soldiers, quieting their fears, encouraging them when they were afraid to jump, guiding them to lifeboats, and helping into lifejackets boys whose hands were too nervous to fasten the strings themselves.

Who were these men of mercy? They were four chaplains of the U.S. Army—one, John Washington, a Catholic priest; another, Alexander P. Goode, a Jew-

... four men calmly went among the soldiers, quieting their fears ...

ish rabbi; and two others, George Fox and Clark Poling, Protestant ministers. These men had joined the U. S. Army during World War II, not to fight, but to help soldiers when they were frightened, and to advise them when they were troubled. And now, in this hour of greatest need, they seemed to be everywhere at once, helping everybody, thinking of nothing but how they could be of service to their fellowmen.

Many were rescued from the sea that day. But the four chaplains were not among them. Amidst all the terror and excitement, few had noticed that the four chaplains had taken off their own life-jackets and given them to men who had none.

As the ship went down, the soldiers in the lifeboats, turning to take a last look at the sinking vessel, saw the four chaplains standing arm in arm, praying.

Who knows what they said? The young Catholic priest may have prayed in Latin, the Protestant ministers in English, and the Jewish rabbi in Hebrew. But whatever their words were, the spirit of what they said must have been the same.

They had all done what their religions had taught them—to help others without any thought of self. They had given help to every man who needed help, without first asking whether he was Protestant, Catholic, or Jew. For these great heroes knew that an American is an American, regardless of his religion; and that all men are brothers and children of the same God.

COLIN KELLY
First Hero of World War II

Nine year old Colin Kelly sat at the edge of his seat, watching his father write the letter. At last, his father signed his name and turned to Colin smiling. "Would you like to read what I wrote to the camp director?"

"Would I!" Colin exclaimed. He knew how pleased his parents had been when he won the honor medal at Camp Carolina that summer. He was excited about what the letter would say.

A grin spread over the lad's face as he read, "Mrs. Kelly and I are delighted that Colin won the medal, and he is proud of his achievement, too. We hope he will go on to strive for high attainments in whatever he attempts."

At this peaceful time in his childhood, Colin did not

*. . . the American dropped three bombs and made
three direct hits.*

dream that one day all America would hear of Colin
Kelly, the first U. S. hero of World War II.

After graduating from West Point in 1937, Colin
was commissioned as an officer in the Army Air Force.
He became the first to pilot a Boeing Flying Fortress
in the Far East.

The Japanese invasion of Pearl Harbor shocked
Kelly, as it did the entire American nation. He vowed
to fight bravely for his country.

In the first two days of the war, Kelly and his crew
moved from field to field in the Philippines, trying to
elude Japanese attack. On the third day, Kelly's Flying
Fortress flew to Clark Field, north of Manila, for a load
of bombs and gasoline. The men had only half finished

loading when the shrill sound of an air raid warning screamed through the air. With time to load only three bombs, Kelly and his men took off in their plane.

"We're heading north," announced Deputy Squadron Leader Kelly. "There's an aircraft carrier we're supposed to sink."

Some time later, Kelly was amazed to sight seven Japanese ships—three transports, three destroyers, and one heavy cruiser. Three Japanese fighter planes were in pursuit. Kelly climbed his big bomber to 20,000 feet. Then, the American dropped three bombs and made three direct hits! The heavy Japanese cruiser Ashigara went up in flames.

On the return to Clark Field, more Japanese fighter planes attacked the Flying Fortress. Enemy machine guns and cannon set Kelly's plane afire. Kelly shouted, "Bail out!" A moment later, the big bird went completely out of control.

Six of Colin's crew bailed out safely, but it was too late for the Captain to follow his own order. His body and the body of an engineer were found near the wreckage.

Colin Kelly's Distinguished Service Cross, awarded after his death, was accepted by his grieving young widow. This young man was one of the many fallen heroes who gave their all for the America they loved and honored.

JOHN F. KENNEDY
Youngest President of the United States

The date was August 2, 1943; the time 2 A.M. PT-Boat 109 had begun its thirty-first mission. Its skipper, John F. Kennedy, stood at the wheel, looking out at a black night which concealed the enemy.

For protection, he had ordered that only one engine be run and that at low speed. At their posts, the crew kept a sharp lookout for enemy targets. But the starless night was too dark; one could see nothing.

Suddenly an alarmed cry rang out. "Ship at two o'clock!" To his horror, Kennedy realized that a Japanese destroyer was heading directly for him. Swiftly touching off the alarm, he shouted, "Sound general quarters!"

It was too late for action. The destroyer smashed

into the PT-Boat, cutting it in two. Breaking apart with a violent pull, PT-109 burst into flames.

The crash threw Kennedy to the deck. For several seconds, he could hardly breathe because of pain.

His half of the PT-Boat was still afloat. When able to see through the darkness, he saw that four of the crew were still hanging on to what was left of the boat. Hoping some of the other men had escaped too, he shouted, "Hello" into the blackness.

Answering shouts confirmed his hope. Six of the crew were swimming in the surrounding waters. One man had been badly burned; another's leg had been hurt in the crash. Kennedy dived into the water, swam towards the first man, and towed him to the float. Then, he swam back for the other man. At last, all eleven exhausted and shaken survivors had been helped aboard the float.

The night passed with agonizing slowness. The situation was desperate. The islands around them teemed with Japanese troops. Meanwhile, their float was slowly sinking. Kennedy decided they had to swim to some island.

Kennedy swam in front of his men, towing McMahon, whose burns had rendered him helpless. After five hours of steady swimming, the crew reached land, by dint of first climbing over some sharp coral reefs which badly cut their feet.

The next four days were a nightmare. As he swam

from island to island in rough seas trying to find help, Kennedy wondered if this was how his life would end. He sharply felt his responsibility for the sick and exhausted men under his command. If he couldn't get help soon, it might be too late. McMahon's burns had become infected. Some of the men were suffering from painful coral cuts.

On the fifth day, Kennedy and another crew member swam to Nauru Island. There, friendly natives heard his story and contacted Americans on a nearby island. The rescue of Kennedy and his ten men was soon accomplished.

Back in America, the news of John F. Kennedy's heroism spread rapidly. For his courageous action, he won the Navy and Marine Medals and the Purple Heart.

In a book John F. Kennedy wrote some time later, *Profiles In Courage,* he said, "A man does what he must . . .in spite of personal consequences, in spite of obstacles and dangers and pressures . . . and that is the basis of all human morality."

John F. Kennedy, was born in Brookline, a suburb of Boston, in 1917. His parents, Joseph Kennedy and Rose Fitzgerald Kennedy, were both descended from Irish Catholic immigrants who fled the 1840 potato famine. Both his grandfathers had been active political leaders; John Fitzgerald—"Honey Fitz" as he was affectionately called—had served several terms as Mayor

*Kennedy swam in front of his men, towing McMahon,
whose burns had rendered his helpless.*

of Boston; Patrick Kennedy had been a state senator in
Massachusetts and a political boss in Boston.

Young Jack, as John Kennedy was nicknamed, was
the second of nine children. He grew up in a home
where religion and politics were given great importance.

The atmosphere in the Kennedy household was one
of warmth and friendly competition. Jack and his older
brother, Joe Jr., competed strenuously. Sometimes it
annoyed Jack that Joe was a better athlete than he. Jack
became an excellent swimmer; he played golf and ten-
nis extremely well, and enjoyed sailing. Home was a
good place during those growing up years.

At 14, Jack entered Choate Academy in Walling-
ford, Connecticut. After graduation, he enrolled at
Princeton, but a siege of jaundice forced him to drop
out. In 1936, he entered Harvard where he majored
in Government and International Relations. At Harvard he injured his back playing football—an injury
that would plague him the rest of his life.

When his father, Joseph Kennedy, became the U. S.
ambassador to England, both Jack and his brother Joe
Jr. became deeply interested in international problems.
In his senior year at Harvard, Jack wrote a thesis in
which he explained why England had not prepared for
war with Nazi Germany. The thesis was published as
a book entitled, *Why England Slept*. Immediately, it
became a best seller. At 23, John F. Kennedy had al-

ready achieved the kind of unusual accomplishment that was to punctuate the rest of his life.

After Jack graduated from Harvard *cum laude* in 1940, he took classes at the Sanford University Graduate Business School, but the work bored him. He dropped out and then spent some time traveling in South America.

Europe was then at war, and the United States was building up its defenses. Kennedy tried to enlist—his brother, Joe, had already received a commission in the Navy. Jack's back injury ruled out Kennedy's first choice, the Air Corps. The Army turned him down, too, because of his back. With characteristic persistence, he decided to strengthen his weak back and did rigorous exerises for five months. Afterwards, he was accepted by the U. S. Navy.

Following the attack on Pearl Harbor by the Japanese, Jack Kennedy applied for active sea duty. Late in 1942, he received an assignment with a PT squadron. He spent six months learning to operate the small craft, and finally was commissioned as an ensign.

Soon after his grueling experience in the South Pacific, Jack contracted malaria. His back, injured again when the PT-Boat was attacked, was giving him constant pain. Sick and weary, he returned to the United States in December, 1943.

At home, another ordeal awaited him. He had to undergo an extremely delicate back operation. Long months of recuperation followed. In the hospital, he received the tragic news that his close brother, Joe Jr., had been shot down over Europe.

When he left the Navy in 1945, John Kennedy was a saddened, sober young man. Now he was faced with an important decision. What would he do with his life? Writing had always interested him, so he became a newspaper reporter.

In 1946, young Kennedy, then 29, ran for Congress and was elected. As a congressman, John Kennedy sponsored bills to help the textile, shoe, and ship building industries in New England. He was re-elected twice.

In 1952, he made an audacious and bold decision for a man of 35. "I've decided," he told lovely young Jacqueline Bouvier whom he had recently met, "to try for a seat in the Senate."

The young woman raised questioning eyes to his. "You mean you want to run against Henry Cabot Lodge?"

He grinned and nodded. "I want to run and I want to win!"

Although Gen. Dwight Eisenhower, the Republican candidate, easily swept to the presidency, Kennedy, a Democrat, beat his Republican opponent by 70,000 votes.

On September 12, 1953, John F. Kennedy married Jacqueline Bouvier. The handsome young Senator and his attractive bride made an unusually striking couple.

But soon after, his back began to trouble him seriously. He resisted crutches until he could not stand without them, and then he decided to undergo another operation.

His wife and family feared another operation. The doctor told them frankly that Jack's life would be in danger. Furthermore, the doctor could not answer for the outcome of the surgery. But Jack had made up his mind. "I'd rather die than spend a lifetime like this," he told his wife. For weeks, he lay without moving. Jacqueline sat constantly at his bedside, and shared his agony. Twice, his condition grew so serious that his wife and his doctors feared for his life.

Hoping a change might help his recovery, the family flew Jack to Florida. But the wound was not healing, and he was returned North to risk still another operation.

Several hours after surgery, the doctor came in to see him. There was a smile on his face as he said, "Well, Senator, you've made it."

"No more crutches?" Jack asked eagerly.

The doctor nodded. "No more crutches," he said. "Your back may give you a bit of trouble now and then, but the worst is over!"

During his recuperation, Jack wrote *Profiles In Courage,* a book which dealt with the political courage of certain American statesmen. The book became a best seller. In 1957, John F. Kennedy won the Pulitzer

Prize for American literature.

In his second Senate term, Kennedy was appointed to the Foreign Relations Committee, one of the most important standing committees of the Senate. Already, the Democrats had begun a movement to nominate him for Vice President.

At the Convention, Kennedy delivered an effective address nominating Adlai Stevenson for President, and through this nationally televised speech, Kennedy's personal charm, sincerity, and force were brought to the attention of the nation.

In an unusual move, Stevenson announced that the race for Vice President was open. John F. Kennedy and Estes Kefauver, Senator from Tennessee, were pitted against each other. When Kennedy realized he had lost, he moved for Kefauver's unanimous nomination.

Kennedy's gracious defeat impressed the members of the Convention. Standing tall and handsome, he thanked all the people who had worked so hard on his behalf. He spent the following months campaigning for Stevenson and Kefauver, and his personal popularity continued to grow apace.

In 1960, John F. Kennedy won the Democratic nomination for President on the first ballot.

From the beginning, there were grave difficulties, the most troublesome of which was the religious issue. No Catholic had ever been elected President of the United States. Not since Al Smith ran in 1928 had a

Catholic even run for President! Prejudice was strong.

Kennedy feared that the voters would not separate his political credo from his religious beliefs.

At a press conference a reporter asked Kennedy "Conceivably there could be a situation in which the dictates of your church and the demands of your country might conflict. In such a case, where would your higher loyalty lie?"

Kennedy did not hesitate. His reply came swiftly and honestly, "I can't act as a private individual does; my responsibility is to my constituents and the Constitution. So if it came to a conflict between the two and not just a personal moral issue, I am bound to act for the interests of the many. It is the obligation of a public servant to defend the Constitution. It is *the* obligation!"

On the touchy civil rights issue, Kennedy declared to an audience made up of Mississippi segregationists, "I accept the Supreme Court decision on school integration as the supreme law of the land."

Kennedy became the youngest President to ever have been elected. He was inaugurated on January 20, 1961, at the age of 44.

In his inauguration speech John Kennedy said, "Let the word go forth from this time and place to friend and foe alike, that the torch has been passed to a new generation of Americans — born in this country, tempered by war, disciplined by a hard and bitter peace, proud of our ancient heritage—and unwilling to wit-

"I am bound to act for the interests of the many."

ness or permit the slow undoing of those human rights to which this nation has always been committed, and to which we are committed today at home and around the world. Let every nation know, whether it wishes us well or ill, that we shall pay any price, bear any burden, meet any hardship, support any friend, oppose any foe to assure the survival and the success of liberty!"

President Kennedy asked for expanded foreign aid and for an intensive space program. He started the Alliance of Progress, and formed the Peace Corps.

The young President was leading an active, progressive administration. The future was promising. Then came November 22, 1963—one of the saddest days in American history. On that terrible day, an assassin shot John F. Kennedy as the President was riding through the streets of Dallas, Texas. Before a stunned nation could grasp the enormity of the tragedy, John Kennedy died in a hospital. He had served two years, ten months, and two days.

His casket was placed inside the vast Rotunda of the Capitol where another assassinated President, Abraham Lincoln, had lain almost one hundred years earlier.

Thousands upon thousands of his countrymen kept vigil all night to view his bier. The nation was plunged into grief, and the entire world mourned.